75

POLITICAL DEVELOPMENT IN LATIN AMERICA:

Instability, Violence,
and Evolutionary Change

Consulting Editor,
LEONARD BINDER,
University of Chicago

WRITTEN UNDER THE AUSPICES OF THE CENTER
FOR INTERNATIONAL AFFAIRS, HARVARD UNIVERSITY

MARTIN C. NEEDLER

University of New Mexico

Political Development in Latin America:

Instability, Violence, and Evolutionary Change

RANDOM HOUSE : NEW YORK

FIRST PRINTING

© Copyright, 1968, by Random House, Inc.
All rights reserved under International and Pan-American Copyright Conventions. Published in New York by Random House, Inc., and simultaneously in Toronto, Canada, by Random House of Canada Limited.
Library of Congress Catalog Card Number: 68–17364
Manufactured in the United States of America
by The Colonial Press, Inc., Clinton, Massachusetts
Typography by Leon Bolognese

TO THE MEMORY OF
KLAUS EPSTEIN

Acknowledgments

The author acknowledges with gratitude the assistance of the Horace H. Rackham Graduate School of the University of Michigan for his appointment as faculty research fellow during the summer of 1964, the Harvard Center for International Affairs for his appointment as research associate during 1965–1966, which alone made completion of the manuscript possible, and the Ford Foundation for its support since 1966 under its project on social revolution in Latin America, directed by Edwin Lieuwen. Special thanks are due to Samuel P. Huntington for his advice and encouragement.

Many individuals, too numerous to mention, made helpful oral comments on earlier versions of various chapters of the manuscript as these were presented as papers at professional meetings and faculty seminars in various places during the course of 1965 and 1966. The author is especially fortunate, in addition, in having had comments on the manuscript, or portions of it, from Luigi Einaudi, Gino Germani, Edwin Lieuwen, Seymour Martin Lipset, Edwin Martin, Lyle McAlister, Francine Rabinovitz, and Walter C. Soderlund. This does not implicate them in the final result, with portions of which I am sure each would disagree.

The author's thanks are also due to Walter Soderlund, whose research is reflected in the data on constitutional stability and military intervention; and also to Richard Loebl and Scott Chamberlain for their research assistance. Finally, the author must express his thanks to the three charming and efficient ladies who typed the manuscript,

Mrs. Jane Tatlock, Mrs. Peggy Byers, and Mrs. J. E. Woodard, Jr.

The American Political Science Review has given permission for the inclusion of Chapter Four, which appeared in an earlier version in its pages.

Contents

POLITICAL DEVELOPMENT IN LATIN AMERICA:

Instability, Violence,
and Evolutionary Change

I
Introduction

A host of conceptual traps and obstacles awaits anyone who tries to discuss "political development." One of the major traps consists of the temptation of confusing the ends to which the processes of political development appear to lead with the normative preferences of the observer, which often derive in turn from an idealized conception of his own society. Thus many participants in the current rather formless discussion centering around the concept of political development might well footnote their use of the term: "When I say political development, I mean democracy; and when I say democracy, I mean current practice in the United States."

This is especially a danger since political development theory is peculiarly an American product, matured and elaborated in an era of American hegemony over much of the globe, when the overwhelming majority of political scientists are American nationals working in the United States. It is thus entirely possible that political development theory could become the vehicle by means of which a dominant world power disguises the ethnocentrism of the political values it seeks to impose, just as the norms of the British political system, at least as these were understood by observers, were so long held up as the ideal to be emulated as much as possible.[1]

Accordingly, when one discusses political development a very high order of conceptual and methodological self-consciousness is required. The following points should thus be taken as prologomena to any discussion of the problem.

In the first place, to assert that political development is

taking place is not to allege that it is inevitable. If development occurs, so does regression, as Samuel Huntington has pointed out. Nevertheless, development represents a possible political process, and, moreover, one that is apparently actually occurring.

Development occurs for several reasons. First, at the level of ideas, a limited number of ideological influences predominate in the world at any one time, and practice tends increasingly to approximate the norms they embody. Second, various social and economic processes go forward which have their own laws of development—for example, economic growth and rationalization, and occupational differentiation—and these processes have specific political correlates. Third, there are regularities in the dynamics of autonomous political processes which have developmental implications; thus, for example, under conditions of party competition there is a tendency for the electorate to expand to its maximum possible size. Because of these and other tendencies, accordingly, there are a priori reasons for believing that political development occurs, even if not inevitably.

The second methodological problem faced in discussions of political development is that of the degree of specificity of content that the concept is given. That is, the term cannot usefully be taken to mean any change which occurs, although it seems at times as though it is used in this way; but neither can it be so narrowly defined as to prescribe only a single predetermined line which change can follow. In other words, "political development" is most fruitfully regarded as describing certain *types* of changes that take place. There are various ways of developing which are alternatives to each other but which nevertheless share common characteristics.

In the third place, it is necessary to distinguish conceptually between the *formal* characteristics of the process of political development, that is, those shown by developing systems in any era, and, on the other hand, the substantive content of the particular process of development occurring during the period under study. Any actual process of development, that is, necessarily shows characteristics typical of processes of development in general and at the same time those typical only of change toward a specific set of norms. This distinction between the formal and the substantive aspects of political development may not have relevance for someone interested only in describing what is actually happening at any moment of time, but is of course essential for any sort of theoretical understanding.

The focus of the present inquiry, accordingly, will be on political development conceived of in terms of changes in political institutions and processes, with reference both to its purely formal character as a process which can occur in any era and to the specific character exhibited by the actual development process in the contemporary world.

In its formal aspect political development will be regarded as the process of transition from one stable equilibrium state of the polity to another, with stability conceived of as the regular functioning of the polity in accordance with the norms it posits for itself.[2] In its substantive aspect, political development in the present era will be regarded as the extension of the polity to include the maximum number of participants taking part in political processes on terms of equality. The two dimensions in which political development can take place today, in this conception, are thus those of constitutional integrity and participation on terms of equality.[3]

In the fourth place, it is necessary to appreciate that the various processes which collectively constitute political development occur in different ways and on different time scales. That is, one has to distinguish between long-range and medium-range effects, between forms of change that are cumulative and others that proceed dialectically, between unilinear and cyclical patterns, as well as between these and purely random effects.

In addition to these general considerations, which must be taken account of in any sophisticated treatment of the question of political development, several procedural decisions have to be made to delimit the scope of an analysis that, like the present one, treats political development in recent and contemporary Latin America. Since the countries of Latin America have, with three exceptions, led an independent existence for a century and a half, it makes most sense to leave to one side consideration of the developmental characteristics of new *states*, which are of importance in a discussion of political development in Africa and Asia; that is, such problems as the establishment of state boundaries, the stipulation of the formal relationship between center and provinces, the achievement of a state machinery staffed by nationals, and so on are not relevant to our present purpose. Some residual questions analogous to these do continue to exist in Latin America, but they no longer constitute the material of the central political issues, as they did in the first years after independence.

The point of departure chosen in the present study is that of a purely political conception of the process of development. A priori, it is thus wholly possible that political development in the sense in which the term is used here should prove to have no systematic relation to the process of economic development; the two might keep pace with each other, they might operate in contradictory directions, or they might have no discernible relationship. This point must be emphasized since some writers appear to use the phrase "political development" as a synonym for the political processes, whatever they may be, which happen to be correlated with economic and social development. Political development, used in this sense, may or may not be the same as political development conceived of in the ways discussed in the following chapters. Whether they are in fact the same is an empirical question and is taken up in Chapter Five.

Perhaps an additional point is in order about the attempts made in subsequent chapters to quantify some of the variables discussed, since this is a question about which so many people have strong feelings. It is true that the use of numerical values gives an appearance of precision that may be misleading, since the sources for the figures given or the methods used in calculating them are less than wholly reliable or the phenomena measured bear only a loose or indirect relation to the reality they are supposed to represent. Because of the various difficulties surrounding the use of numerical values, the author intends that his use of them be suggestive rather than conclusive. Nevertheless, they do perform a valuable function in helping the observer to choose among theoretical alternatives which are a priori equally possible and in directing his attention to otherwise unsuspected relationships.

At the same time, the author is painfully aware that because of the incomplete nature of the data that are available or can now be derived, what is written here will surely be superseded rapidly as the body of available data becomes more complete and as resourceful minds refine the theoretical questions to which the data can be made to yield answers. This study is thus intended to be no more than an early stage of a succession of increasingly exact or comprehensive approximations.

It seems likely, for example, that significant regularities will be perceived more readily when data are available that can reveal not only the state of a variable at a given point of time[4] but also the rates and directions of change. At present this is possible with respect to only a limited number of types of data.

Nevertheless, it is clear that the problem is not that of finding "causes" of relative political underdevelopment in Latin America in qualitative terms, for the literature is rich in theses about such causal factors, cogently and often brilliantly stated.[5] As Arthur Whitaker writes, "It is not that the 'causes' which have been assigned are wrong, still less that there are not enough of them, for the main trouble with them is that they are too numerous. They tell both too little and too much." [6]

The intention here is to introduce data in order to answer "theory-relevant" questions, but the concentration throughout is on theory. Thus this approach contrasts with the traditionally more prevalent one of maintaining the discussion on a theoretical level throughout while making no attempt to use empirical data to discriminate between equally plausible theoretical possibilities. It also contrasts with the emerging tendency to proceed by first accumulating all the quantifiable data that come most readily to hand, that most resemble data already collected by colleagues, and that are amenable to procedures of collection that have become institutionalized and funded—and only subsequently, if at all, attempting to discern their theoretical significance.

Because of the complexities of the subject, the author has thought it advisable to approach it from several directions in turn, using a variety of techniques of analysis. Thus the study takes up in sequence the problems of stability and instability, violence, the relations between social and political change, and the strategies by which change is consciously brought about.

II
Stability and Instability

One:
AN ANALYTIC FRAMEWORK

The focus of attention in this chapter is not on political development conceived of as the progressive attainment of a high-participation democratic or near-democratic polity, but on systemic political change in general. After an examination of the dimensions in which systemic political change takes place, the discussion of stability and instability focuses on the understanding of political processes in Latin America at a rather high level of generality. Subsequent chapters will then deal with specific questions raised here as they relate to the problem of political development.

If one asks under what conditions a polity can be said to be functioning stably, he finds himself confronted by a great wealth of thinking on the subject. If one replaces the question "What factors make for stability in the polity?" by its behavioral correlate "Why do individuals act as the stable functioning of the polity requires?" one is in effect asking, "Why does an individual accept and obey constituted authority?" And yet the history of political thought consists principally, after all, of a set of answers to just this question.

The variety of bases for civil obedience which are suggested by the classical literature seems to be exhausted by the formulation that individual subjects obey established government because (1) it does not occur to them to do anything else (essentially Hume's point); (2) they have no power to change things (in part, Bentham); (3) the system gratifies needs they feel (social contract theory); or (4) they believe it right to do so, even where they receive no palpable benefits from obedience.[1] On this fourth point, one needs to distinguish between justifications of obedience (a) proposed for specific political systems—for example, rule by divine right, by the specially gifted, or by democratic majorities—and (b) those available to justify *any* existent system, such as the conception of actual government as by definition the cumulation of past wisdom and experience, as in portions of Burke; as the current expression of immanent Reason in history, as in Hegel; or as necessarily willed by God, as in some of the medieval and Reformation theorists.

The list given seems exhaustive and appears in fact to comprise all the logical possibilities, given moderately rationalist and hedonist assumptions about human nature.

It should be noted, however, that two of these sets of putative bases for obedience, those included in categories (1) and (4b) above, apply to any polity, once it has established itself. The factors comprehended in these categories can thus operate to *maintain* stable systems but are not relevant to the problem of why a given institutional formula *becomes* stable, nor to the problem of why it begins to undergo change. To explain the genesis of change and instability, therefore (assuming that the list given above *is* exhaustive), we must resort to the factors which comprise the other categories—(2), (3), and (4a)—and say that a system of government is stable when it reflects the informal distribution of power, when it gratifies the needs of those subject to it, or when its ideological bases are accepted by them—or some combination of these three.

It should further be stipulated that although the discussion thus far has been couched in terms of the individual's relations to the polity, the stability of the latter is determined not by support or withdrawal of support on the part of only one or two individuals, but of numbers of individuals over certain minimum quantitative levels.

In order to make use of this set of principles about individual attitudes at the level of the whole political system, a model of the polity can be constructed which shows the relations among "system components" which they posit. No attempt is being made here to develop an all-purpose model of the political system, as is done by some current authors.[2] The diagram rather concretizes the individual attitudes described—that is, one's belief that his interests are being satisfied by government policy, one's belief that the government's title to office is indeed valid, and the congruence between the authority relations established by the constitutional system and the power relations which actually obtain in the society.

It should be noted that we are holding in abeyance all the "great issues" of political thought by treating the theses propounded by the great doctrinaires not as mutually exclusive dogmas but as descriptions of social reality which may describe that reality more accurately or more comprehensively at some times and places than at others, but which can be subsumed by a more general statement that is at the same time not too general to be without pragmatic value. Thus one can speak of the informal power or dominance relations within society (as distinct from the distribution of "powers" in the formal constitutional system) without specifying if these are based on force of numbers, control of the means of production, habitual "deference" of the lower orders, or some other factor.

The great questions in the philosophy of history are treated similarly. It is assumed here, for example, that individuals can lend support to a government, or withdraw support from it, on the basis of its satisfaction of either their "interests" or their ideal aspirations—not that acknowledgment of one excludes acknowledgment of the other or that one is necessarily but the reflection of the other.

In choosing to proceed in this way and not commit himself to one or the other pole of any set of grand alternatives, the author is of course choosing a general philosophical position as well as a mode of analysis. No answer is also an answer, as the Germans say.

We now analyze this model of the polity in detail.

In the *official* sector of the polity, on the right-hand side of Figure 1, there are three elements: (1) the structure of public policy; (2) the formal structure of authority—that is, governmental machinery and the electoral system; and (3) the "official" ideology.

The *unofficial* sector consists of what I must apologize for calling "groups," which have felt interests and ideologies and are related to each other by a structure of dominance relations. These three facets of the structure of the unofficial sector parallel those of the official sector; that is, the dimensions of each are interest and interest gratification (in policy), ideology, and power-and-authority relationships.[3]

A stably functioning polity is one in which there is a limited set of patterns of normal behavior, which recur predictably in given sets of circumstances. The decisions of legitimate officeholders are routinely given effect by lesser officials; established procedures are followed; laws are generally obeyed. These regularities would clearly be disrupted if structures entailing mutually exclusive patterns of behavior with respect to the central features of political life coexisted in the same political system. That is, a certain amount of tension between the demands of conflicting roles is clearly inevitable; but at the same time, there are limits to the amount of such tension that a system can support and remain stable. The problem can, however, be kept within manageable limits if one talks in terms of an ideal-typical perfectly stable polity in which perfect compatibility among normal behaviors exists.

Let us now return to our original statement that individual subjects obey government because (1) it does not occur to them to do anything else; (2) they have no power to change things; (3) government gratifies the needs they

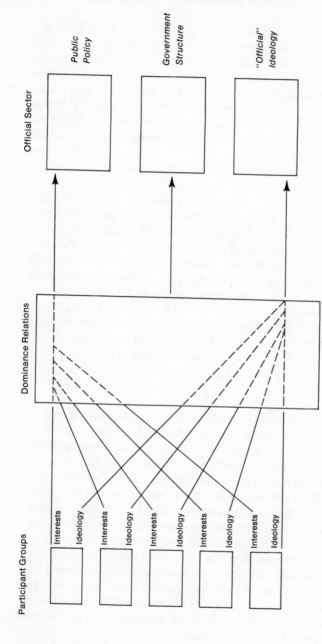

FIGURE 1. *The Political System*

Arrows indicate the principal relations of compatibility necessary for perfectly stable functioning.

feel; or (4) they believe it right to do so. Translated into terms of system variables under conditions of systemic stability, that statement would now read: In a perfectly stable polity, particular interests and particular ideologies, as mediated through the set of dominance relations, are compatible, respectively, with public policy and with the "public philosophy," while the structure of dominance relations in the society is itself compatible with the structure of public authority.

It must be stressed that particular interests and ideologies do not necessarily have a direct relation to their public counterparts, policy and public philosophy respectively, but are mediated through the system of dominance relations. That is, public ideology may merely replicate the class ideology of the ruling group, and public policy, its interests. Or informal power may be equilibrated so that all groups share public authority, public policy represents the resultant of demands competing on equal terms, and the public ideology is consistent with all group ideologies; or one group may dominate by virtue of a strategic position which enables it to hold a balance of power and derive more benefit than its "fair share" from public policy; and so on.

We turn next to a consideration of systemic change in the polity—change, that is, which consists not merely of the motions performed by the system functioning as its norms suppose it should, but of change which entails the transformation of the system into a system of another type. The discussion here is limited to change within the polity itself. That is, change introduced into the political system through modifications in one or other of its components may certainly originate in the demographic or economic or cultural subsystems of the total social system of which the polity is only one aspect. Nothing written here should be construed so as to deny this patent truth. However, the extrapolitical origins of political change will be treated here as "secular"; change interests us here only after it is introduced into the political system.

An examination of the types of systemic changes which can occur suggests two theses about the nature of this kind of change: (1) change in the polity can be introduced into it through any of its components rather than originating exclusively with any one of them; (2) there is a tendency to compatibility among system components so that regardless of where change originates, it tends either to modify all elements of the polity toward consistency with it or else to be eliminated from the system, with the ultimate outcome depending on the properties of the specific change in question.

If these two contentions are true (and evidence is introduced below to show that they are), then the following types of change are possible:

1. An increase or decrease in the set of groups which participate in the polity
2. Changes in an already included group's conception of its interests, or in its ideology
3. Change in relative positions of political dominance

These could then be expected to affect the three "official" elements of the polity. Or the latter may be modified directly by

4. Changes which do not originate within the specific political system itself or in related dimensions of the total social system but in other political systems, including the system of interstate relations; that is, changes that are imposed directly on the polity by foreign influence, pressure, or conquest
5. Changes generated from within the "official" sector without a compelling secular origin; that is, changes deriving from autonomous decisions of the rulers and not forced upon them

By showing that each of these types of change does in fact take place, we will be demonstrating that change can be introduced into the polity through any of its components, as provisionally assumed above; and we will then be in a position to see under what circumstances the tendency to consistency among the components of the system comes into operation and when that tendency is frustrated.

Type 1 Change

The first type of change takes place by addition or subtraction in the set of groups participating in the polity. It may come about through the creation of new socioeconomic classes, for example, as a result of evolution in the processes of material production, distribution, and exchange. With the growth of towns, a class of burghers develops; with the introduction of the factory system, the proletariat is created; and so on.

This type of change need not have immediate secular origins, however, but may develop as the indirect result of secular change which is mediated through another element of the polity and thus itself reflect the tendency toward consistency postulated above. For example, the change in the structure of dominance relations of the then Union of South Africa that resulted in the hegemony of the Afrikaner Nationalists led to the effective exclusion from participation in politics (in the narrow sense) of the so-called Cape Coloured by their removal from the voting roll.

Change mediated from outside by other elements of the polity not only may result in the inclusion or exclusion of already existing groups; it also may be the cause of the *creation* of new social groups. This point should be stressed since it would otherwise be plausible to assume that the creation of new groups is exclusively a function of economic or demographic processes, which is not, in fact, the case. Adoption of the goal of universal free and compulsory education has been particularly significant here. Of course, it made possible the full participation of groups which had previously existed only on the margins of the polity—for example, industrial workers—where a literacy requirement represented the threshold to participation. But general public education has also created a whole new "estate" of schoolteachers, a factor of central significance for the politics of some countries.

Chile is perhaps the leading example. There the public education law is enforced (which is not always the case elsewhere in Latin America), and an education system has been created generally regarded as the finest in the Hemisphere below the Rio Grande. The estate of teachers created by the law for some time gave its allegiance principally to the Radical party, which was until very recently the crucial party in Chilean governments (as its equivalent used to be in France) and set the tone for the whole system. Thus in the Chilean case a change in public policy made possible the participation of preexisting groups but also created a new participant group. The informal system of power relations then changed from one of competitive equality between two classes of almost equal status (urban businessmen and professionals versus rural landowners) to one of equilibrium among a range of classes and subclasses, with the new groups of teachers and public workers eventually holding a balance of power.[4]

Type 2 Change

The second type of change takes place not in the existence or inclusion of groups but in the directions in which they act politically, resulting from changes in their conceptions of their interests or in their ideologies.

A striking example of this type of change is afforded by the shift to support of Nazism during the late Weimar period made by Protestant lower middle class elements in Germany that had previously supported, in the main, the two Liberal parties. This is not the place to examine the problem at length, of course. It is of central significance in understanding what happened in Germany, however, to appreciate that, while the Catholic Center party maintained its position fairly well through the Depression and the other events which contributed to the rise of the Nazis and the Social Democratic party decreased in strength by losing primarily to the Communists, who after all represented a more extreme view of the same basic world orientation, the Liberal parties were completely wiped out, their support going largely to a party whose views were the absolute antithesis of their own. The writer would suggest that this occurred because extreme adversity did not in itself undermine commitment to either Catholic or Marxist premises, which not only explain the world but also explicitly reconcile their adherents to adversity as part of the scheme of things but temporary and subordinate to the eventual attainment of great goods. Liberalism, on the other hand, is eminently optimistic and, in stressing the individual's responsibility for his own success or failure rather than regarding him as primarily a participant in a larger organic entity, puts a severe burden on his adjustment to the world during a time of prolonged adversity.

As an essentially fair-weather ideology, that is, Liberalism could not withstand the protracted storm of the Depression, and most of its votaries turned to a faith that was the diametric opposite of Liberalism in offering precisely the abdication of individual responsibility and the denial of individually assessed merit. Because of its numbers and strategic position in the political system, the transfer of the ideological loyalties of the Protestant lower middle class then made possible the transformation of the entire political system.

Type 3 Change

Change in the system of dominance relations is, in effect, revolution, although that term is applied so generally that it is just as well to use it sparingly. Change of this type often, but not always, entails the use of violence. An example of such a change without violence would be provided by a situation in which two parties existed, dedicated to totally different visions of society and supported by two different ethnic groups. Over time the minority party could become a permanent majority because the group from which it drew support had a higher birth rate than its rival. This simple demographic fact, in other words, could lead to a complete reversal in dominance relations.

Type 4 Change

Change in elements of the polity can originate not only in secular changes in systems (economic, demographic, and

so on) coextensive with the polity, but also in other political systems to which it relates. Examples of such change
would be a change in government structure imposed as a
result of foreign conquest, for example, the "democratization" of Germany and Japan following World War II or
the introduction of its own forms of government within a
colony by a colonial power; the imposition of a policy from
outside by means of conquest or the threat of sanctions, as
in the case of the reparations exacted from Germany after
World War I; or the transmission of ideas which seems
to occur from a country of higher prestige to one of lower
prestige (higher or lower in the eyes of the lower-prestige
country itself).

Type 5 Change

Changes introduced deliberately by those in authority, like
externally induced changes, need not derive from changes
going forward in other subsystems of the social system but
may in this sense be arbitrary. Like externally induced
changes, again, they can persist only if they happen for
some reason to be consonant with the informal realities,
or if these can be modified so as to be harmonious with
them and thus to support and maintain them. If neither of
these occur, then the imposed modes of behavior will be
rejected when force is no longer available to maintain
them, after the dictator or the ruling group is removed by
abdication, death, or revolution.

Thus Richard Cromwell's rejection of the offer to succeed his father as ruler of England, given the context of
seventeenth-century ideas, appeared to leave the achievement of political stability dependent on the restoration of
the legitimate monarchy.

As is suggested by the examples cited, change in the
informal sector of the polity, once it has been able to
register its effect on the system of dominance relations,
experiences little difficulty in then transforming the "official" sector of the political system. Change which *originates* in the official sector, however, seems much less likely
to be able to modify the unofficial elements of the polity

into conformity with it. It stands a greater chance, therefore, of being rejected by the political system.

Thus modifications in government introduced during a period of alien rule may be abandoned when national independence is achieved, as is occurring today in many of the former colonial states. Policies followed under constraint may, similarly, be abandoned when the constraint is lifted.

Change introduced in the official sector has a better prospect of permanence, accordingly, if it happens for some reason to be consistent with preexisting informal reality or if it is accompanied by structural change in the informal sector. Thus although the future of West German democracy may not yet be assured, it is certainly brighter because the Junkers no longer exist as a class, as they did within the formal democracy of Weimar.

The Russians, conditioned by Marxist ways of thinking to give primacy to questions of social structure and dominance relations, deliberately modified the class structure in their half of Germany (by the expulsion and liquidation of individuals) to try to guarantee the permanence of the political changes they made.

The further possibility exists that change in the formal sector of the policy of external origin is not forced upon it, to be tolerated and then rejected as soon as possible, but is imported voluntarily. The newly introduced change may succeed in transforming unofficial reality into harmony with it; if it does not and yet is maintained—because, for some reason, no alternatives are acceptable—then a condition of continuing disharmony in the polity is created. How this type of situation may come about will be discussed subsequently.

We are now in a position to distinguish among three stability states of the polity. A polity is *stable* if it has been functioning over a long period of time in keeping with its set of official prescriptions; it is *evolving* if changes are taking place in the direction of increasing harmony, that is, consistency, among the components of the polity;[5] it is in a state of *permanent instability* if it neither functions as it is officially supposed to nor develops toward greater harmony among its elements, which remain inconsistent with each other.[6]

The concept of permanent instability accurately characterizes the political life of most of Latin America during the greater part of the postindependence period.[7] Around the turn of the century and for some time afterward, a substantial degree of stability existed, as will be discussed below, and today there appear to be one or two stable, and an increasing number of evolving, systems. Nevertheless, for most of the period the dominant condition seems to have been that of permanent instability.

On the basis of the foregoing discussion the writer would propose that this peculiar character of Latin American political life is due to a continuing disharmony between the formal structure of government, the behavior it requires, and the ideas which sustain it, on the one hand, and informal sociopolitical realities, summarized by the set of dominance relations, on the other.

That is, the stable functioning of the polity is not possible because the norms established for it require behavior patterns inconsistent with those required by the informal distribution of power and the social realities on which the latter is based.

Yet if this is so, why is it that formal political structures are not brought into harmony with the informal realities by the normal mechanisms for the reduction of inconsistencies between the different behavior patterns of the individual? Why should instability be permanent, rather than a transitional phase lasting only until the tendency to consistency brings about a new equilibrium?

The answer lies in the fact that, for most of the postindependence period, no internationally respectable alternatives to the forms of government organization prescribed in the constitutions of the area, or to the general principles of political ideology that they reflect, have managed to maintain themselves for any length of time. Occasionally, some style of government at variance with the liberal-democratic consensus has survived for a time in a European country and provided one of Latin America's dictators with an opportunity to appear fashionable: Francisco Solano López copies Napoleon III, or Getúlio Vargas proclaims a corporate state; Fidel Castro announces himself a Marxist-Leninist, or Jânio Quadros asks the parliament to vote him the powers "that de Gaulle has in France." But these deviations have been atypical and ephemeral; typically the norms of democracy, liberty, and constitutional government have been professed, and the appropriate procedures followed, at least as rituals, no matter how great their lack of consonance with social and political reality.

This is so because Latin America has always been ideologically part of the "Atlantic Community." Her communciations networks are integrated with those of Europe and North America, for example; the pages of the Latin American press are fed principally by dispatches from UPI and Agence France Presse. The intellectual leaders of the area are to be found in France or the United States as much as they are in their own countries. They have attended North American universities. The regional political organization is dominated by the United States and has its headquarters in Washington; and the United States continually attempts to propagate democratic ideology in the Hemisphere, by its words, if only intermittently by its deeds. At the same time, social realities are quite at variance with the requirements of democratic ideology. All citizens are to be equal before the law, and all should participate equally in government; but drastic sociopolitical inequalities permeate the society, based not only on extreme inequality in the distribution of wealth, but also on "racial" criteria, especially in the countries with large Indian populations.

If the systemic incompatibilities posited by the writer between official "public" ideology and sociopolitical realities exist, then their attitudinal correlates should be discernible as ambivalence or inconsistency in the attitudes of individual Latin Americans, between attitudes explicitly "about" formal political ideology, on the one hand, and either attitudes toward actual political behavior or reports of behavior itself, on the other; ". . . side by side with each other in complete disaccord, the tenets of an ideology and the 'beliefs' and actual behavior of day-to-day life." [8]

There is indeed supporting evidence from the opinion survey data that are available of a dichotomy precisely of this type. Daniel Goldrich has found that among Panamanian high school students of middle and upper class backgrounds "there is a relatively strong belief that political democracy is desirable and that national elections are meaningful." [9] And yet this is in a country whose realities Goldrich describes as follows:

> Politics in Panama has been characterized by fairly casual changes of government through revolution, coup, extensive manipulation of the electoral system, and even assassination. These upheavals have been essentially insignificant so far as concerns any change in basic social or economic policies or the perspectives of the decision-makers. There has been no substantial program to relieve the poverty of the masses, and welfare programs and social legislation exist only at a low degree of development. Extreme corruption has formed a constant element in the picture at all levels.[10]

A similar inconsistency in attitudinal data, this time from Mexico, confronted the authors of *The Civic Culture*. They found that Mexico rated lower than the other four (non-Latin American) countries surveyed "in the frequency with which impact and significance are attributed to government and in its citizens' expectations of equal and considerate treatment at the hands of the bureaucracy and police. At the same time, the frequency with which Mexicans express pride in their political system is considerably higher than that of the Germans or Italians." [11]

Especially interesting is "another striking inconsistency. . . . high frequencies in subjective political competence are coupled with the lowest frequencies of all five countries in political performance (as measured by political information scores, voluntary association membership, and political activity)." [12]

On the basis of the interpretation of Latin American politics developed previously one would expect that anomalies, inconsistencies, and ambivalence similar to those revealed by the Mexican and Panamanian data can be found in the other countries of Latin America, due less to peculiar national circumstances or temporary conditions than to underlying structural characteristics of the politics of the area.

This view appears supported by fragmentary evidence now becoming available from other attitude surveys. A survey being conducted under the direction of Alex Inkeles, for example, has found among lower class Argentine and Chilean respondents a wide gap between subjective sense of political efficacy and reports of actual political participation similar to that found by Almond and Verba in Mexico.

It is instructive to review the history of independent Latin America to see how the patterns of "permanent instability" originated and have been maintained.

The Latin American countries have been since independence in a peculiarly anomalous position. In the first place, independence itself came, for most of them, more or less by accident rather than as an expression of changing social realities. Very crudely and briefly put, after Napoleon invaded Spain, legitimate colonial authority ceased to exist in the Spanish-speaking countries, which refused to accept the viceroys sent out by the Corsican. By the time Napoleon was overthrown, however, the former colonies had become used to running their own affairs and refused to return to their former status. In social and political terms, the only change which took place was the substitution of the social elite of Spaniards born in America for a set of rulers sent out from the Peninsula.

What is worthy of note, however, is that, despite Bolívar's attempts to create a set of ideas of legitimacy that would make possible structures of government reflecting the systems of class and caste distinction that continued to dominate society, Latin Americans persisted in looking abroad for their sources of inspiration, especially to France and the United States.[13] The dominant political ideas in Latin America during the early independence period were undoubtedly those of the *philosophes* and of contemporary United States thinkers.

Once the ideas about political legitimacy that had informed the colonial system—that authority derives from the rights of birth, and ultimately from God's grace—were swept away, the only internationally respectable alternative was the egalitarian and individualist republicanism which was the message of the French Revolution and, or so it seemed from a distance, of the American Revolution.

Most of the new constitutions were based on republican and democratic premises and often borrowed phraseology directly from the Constitution of the United States. But the gap between legal norm and social reality was too great for behavior to bridge. Accordingly, the actual exercise of power could be plausibly legitimated neither in the traditional colonial terms, which had been rejected by the act of proclaiming independence itself, nor in the newly available terms of equality and the rights of man. The result was that the possession of political authority lacked the support in informal attitudes and behavior which alone could make possible its regular and peaceful transfer, or even its routine acceptance.

This is the explanation of the peculiar fate of Latin American constitutions, which are verbally honored, repeatedly cited, and promulgated anew to justify each revolution retroactively, yet have no effect on fundamental political reality. The formula usually used by scholars in the attempt to account for this phenomenon is that in Latin America constitutions represent sets of aspirations, not serious prescriptions for behavior. This is doubtless true, but there has been little tendency to ask why it should be so, and what saying that it is implies.[14]

Under the conditions of this "legitimacy vacuum," therefore, all that remained was reliance on naked force, and the conditional loyalty of contenders' supporters was secured principally only by particularistic ties[15] and hope of personal gain. Weberian charisma could not constitute the foundation of new systems of institutionalized legitimacy because trial by arms was the only possible adjudicator between rival charismatic claims. Although they are beginning to give way gradually under the impact of forces discussed below, the leading characteristics of Latin American politics remain to this day personalism, frequent resort to force, the spoils system and the prevalence of graft, and the particularistic character of relations of solidarity.

It should be noted that the characteristics of Hispanic culture, while not determining (as Chapter Three makes clear), are also relevant here in that Hispanic attitudes seem to be peculiarly able to support situations in which professed ideals are at variance with everyday realities. Spain is the country that gave birth to Don Quixote, after all.

Two:
HISTORY AS DEVELOPMENT

If, as the foregoing analysis suggests, instability results from the maintenance, after their implantation by processes of cultural diffusion, of public ideologies and sets of institutions incompatible with the attitudes and dominance relations of the informal sector of the polity, then the achievement of stability requires that the two sets of elements be brought into mutual harmony. It should be stressed that it is not normally feasible in Latin America today to modify public belief systems, and thus the sets of formal institutions which these support, except to even greater consonance with internationally respectable ideology. Thus stability on the basis of a nondemocratic official ideology is not possible. Attempts to achieve such stability are made from time to time but today they are bound to fail.[1] Short of a totally democratic stability, there can only be either a state of permanent instability or an unstable state steadily modified in the direction of greater fidelity to democratic norms. It has been repeatedly made evident that politically conscious Latin Americans accept without question the norms of the complex of democratic public ideas, at least *as* norms.

This is demonstrated, for example, by the presence of

bad conscience among military officers who stage coups
d'état today. Their first concern is almost invariably to set
a date for new elections and to justify the coup to domestic and foreign opinion in terms of democratic ideology.[2]
Until quite recently, the general pattern was for a coup
d'état to result in a government in office for an indefinite
period and perhaps until it itself was overthrown, headed
by the leader of the successful insurrection, who had thus
earned his right to serve as president. An election in which
the leader of the coup was unopposed or only nominally
opposed for the presidency might be held as a matter of
form, but the issue would never be in question. This pattern is occasionally reproduced in Latin America today, for
example (up to the time of writing), after the Argentine
coup of 1966; but as evolution in a democratic direction
has become more widespread, this pattern has become
exceptional. In fifteen out of the nineteen coups d'état
which took place during the decade 1955–1964, the overthrown government was instead succeeded by a provisional
government charged with making preparations for elections
within a limited period of time.[3]

This situation bears some contemplation. A military
group has made itself master of the country, yet it under-
takes to relinquish power almost immediately. The striking
thing about this pattern of behavior is not that the results
of the ensuing elections may sometimes not be respected,
or that they may be conducted in a partial manner, but
that the hold of the norms of democratic ideology is so
great, even on the perpetrators of a successful coup d'état,
that any situation other than the restoration of a formally
constitutional government issuing from free elections is
simply not thinkable. The Idea, if one may so express it,
holds sway. Powerful self-interested motives may cause
deviations from the behavior it prescribes, and it may seem
ludicrous that the perpetrators of an extraconstitutional
seizure of power can speak with such apparent sincerity of
the reimposition of constitutional norms, but there can
be no doubt that leading political actors do indeed go to
considerable lengths, and do act against what appears to be

in their immediate interest, in order to try to bring their behavior into conformity with constitutional prescription.

It has perhaps not been sufficiently appreciated that a military seizure of power does not mean the imposition of rule by brute force. Normally, the structure of law, the permanent officials, the courts remain as before. Typically, the regulations governing seniority are strictly adhered to in assigning junta, cabinet, and subcabinet positions to military officers. The interventionists regard themselves as acting on behalf of the national interest and the maintenance of the integrity of the constitution, against a government which was itself the violator of legality and constitutional norms. Thus the coup does not entail the abandonment of those norms and the ideology they embody. The existence of the institution of the military coup thus, paradoxically, in no way nullifies the point that democratic and constitutional norms are generally accepted by politically conscious Latin Americans. The writer suspects that the apparently exceptional case of Cuba under Castro, which will be dealt with later in another connection, will prove, similarly, to be only a temporary aberration.

Given the pervasiveness of democratic ideology, then, long-term stability in Latin America today can only be democratic stability; it can come only as a result of the modification of relations among classes and groups so that informal reality can become faithful to the political forms and their supporting ideas to which there has been no effective alternative.

In terms of the distinctions made above, if a polity is not stable, it can escape permanent instability only by becoming an "evolving" system. There is all the difference in the world, for example, between a country which uses a literacy requirement for voting in order to disenfranchise an Indian population which it makes no attempt to educate and one in which the education and integration of the Indian population receive priority precisely so that Indians too may participate in the system of representation.

In countries in which ethnic and economic realities have produced great social distinctions, it is possible to incorporate democratic political norms only where the operating political regimes regard themselves avowedly as transitional and undertake both to transform social reality in an egalitarian sense and to give increasing substance to the political ideals which the polity posits. Mexico is, of course, the prime example of an evolving polity in the area, since its social policy is directed precisely at the creation of conditions which can support political democracy and its political system is modifying itself steadily to approximate increasingly the ideal posited. It is surely only in following the Mexican way—that is, by accepting temporarily less than ideally democratic modes of operation which are still consonant with social realities, while at the same time strenuously reforming those realities so that ever more democratic political practices can be adopted—that political stability can be achieved by nonegalitarian societies in a democratic age.

It should be noted that in such an "evolving" polity, as in those functioning under conditions of "permanent instability," various institutions appropriate to a country where stable democracy has already been achieved are nonfunctional or even dysfunctional. The geographic decentralization of power may support democracy under conditions of a stable constitutional order, for example, but is likely to impede its introduction elsewhere. Thus former President Emilio Portes Gil has complained that federalism was adopted in Mexico in slavish imitation of United States forms without regard for Mexican realities; in Mexico it has become a cover for fraud, peculation, and petty dictatorship.

It was at one time believed in the United States that the reason for political instability in Latin America was the lack of discipline in the armies of the area. If discipline could be improved and armies professionalized, it was thought, military intervention in politics would be less likely. The United States had the opportunity to act on this belief when, as a result of circumstances which need not concern us here, it assumed protectorates over Haiti, the Dominican Republic, and Nicaragua early in the

twentieth century and occupied those countries with
Marines. Before withdrawing its forces, the United States
organized and trained efficient, disciplined, and professional
constabulary units of a size adequate only for the preservation of domestic order. It soon proved, however, that although it was possible to train subordinate officers and the
rank and file to obey commands from above, it was not
possible to guarantee respect for civilian authority in the
commanders of the constabulary. Shortly after the withdrawal of United States troops, power was seized by the
minister responsible for the constabulary in Nicaragua,
Anastasio Somoza, and by the Dominican commander,
Rafael Trujillo; the chief officers of the Garde d'Haïti con-
tented themselves with playing the role of Great Elector,
without—with one or two exceptions—assuming office
themselves. Ironically, the Dominican and Nicaraguan
constabularies had been so well-trained and had been made
so efficient that organized resistance to the new dictatorships was impossible, and Somoza and Trujillo were each
removed eventually only by assassination.

The writer has also taken the position that the introduction of a civil service based on examinations, merit pro-
motions, tenure, and so on, is, similarly, inappropriate for
most of the Latin American countries in their present
stage of development.[4] Unless the importance of social
class is drastically reduced in Latin American life—for
example, in the equalization of educational opportunity—
then the whole apparatus of "good government" civil service reform becomes just another mode of preserving class
rule and obstructing social change. With such a civil service
system, innovating leaders find that they have to contend
not only with political opposition in the legislature and the
country but also with obstruction and sabotage within the
government apparatus itself, just as much as with a civil
service deliberately recruited from the possessing classes.
"The revolution above, the counterrevolution below" was
the way a top-ranking permanent official described to the
writer what was happening to the reform program of the
junta that took power in Ecuador during 1963. A Jackson-

ian spoils system at least affords the possibility that officials will agree with the policy goals of the incoming government.

The British left awoke to this phenomenon in their own country some time ago. The British civil service has been based on competitive examination for some time; this reduced the fact of upper class and upper middle class domination of the government service only marginally, however. In the first place, the examinations given stressed humanistic studies, and an ideology was developed (the need for generalists, and so on) to justify this emphasis; yet competence in these areas depended on attendance at schools to which admission was until 1947 predominantly limited in terms of class and wealth. In the second place, admission to the ranks of the higher civil service depended on performance not only on written examinations but also on extended personal interviews, in which the criteria used were clearly heavily biased in favor of those of higher social origin.[5] One gets a feeling for how recent the conversion to authentic egalitarianism in the public service has been, even as a principle, by recalling that it was less than a century ago that the British actually abolished the purchase of military commissions.[6]

One who takes the view that the ideas flowing into Latin America from North America and Europe have not been consonant with Latin American social reality and have led to instability because of the difficulties preventing reconciliation of the two must make clear that he should not be identified with such apologists for tyranny as Vallenilla Lanz, who wrote that "Caesarian democracy" is peculiarly fitted to the realities of Hispanic America.[7] The drawbacks of "Caesarian democracy" are surely well known and need not be summarized here. The point is rather that although the function of the ideal is to indicate in what way the actual should be changed, if too wide a gulf develops between reality and the normative pattern, the effort to make the one conform to the other is given up as too great; the norm must then yield every hope of influencing actual behavior, which is abandoned to sheer cynicism, force, and considerations of short-range self-interest.

The role of imported ideas in maintaining sets of official ideals that do not grow out of the underlying structures of group interests, attitudes, and positions of power (and thus are potentially in conflict with them) appears clear enough as it relates to the "permanent instability" of an era of democratic norms. At the same time, it should be noted that there was a period during the history of postindependence Latin America during which the temporary ascendancy of nonliberal ideas in the prestigious countries of Western Europe made possible the establishment of a peaceful and stable order in parts of Latin America despite the persistence of markedly nondemocratic social structures.

Political scientists generalizing about the whole range of Latin American political life (and the present writer acknowledges his share of blame in this) have tended to overlook the special character of this era of stability, which extended for some countries for a period of several decades beginning in the 1880s or 1890s. José Medina Echevarría has recently suggested a reevaluation of this period in the context of the current concern with problems of development.[8]

The point has also been noted by Edwin Lieuwen, who relates the breakdown of early twentieth-century stability to the emergence of new social groups.[9] Samuel P. Huntington has also pointed out that the early twentieth century was a period of greater stability than the mid-twentieth century, as measured by the frequency of military intervention in politics.[10] It is instructive to review—at least for some of the larger Latin American countries—how stability was achieved during this epoch and how it was lost.

Before Porfirio Díaz resumed his interrupted thirty-year rule in 1884, Mexico had been the most turbulent and chaotic country in Latin America. Yet just before the end of his period in office, in 1909, Mexico could borrow all the money she wanted at 5 percent,[11] which for that era was a sign of maximum success, and Theodore Roosevelt went so far as to refer to Díaz as the greatest statesman of his time.

Díaz promoted what he and his contemporaries regarded

as progress in Mexico, first establishing "order" as a pre-requisite. Yet it would be unfair to Díaz to interpret his achievement as resting on bayonets alone or to view him as simply another personalist *caudillo* who ruled by ma-nipulating people and weapons, for a large element in Díaz's success was his manipulation of symbols. In the words of Howard F. Cline: "Díaz's rule was not pinned together by bayonets, but by ideas." [12] And he adds: "Far from being out of step with their time, the Porfirian *cien-tíficos* were in the main streams of world opinion." [13]

The philosophical basis of the Díaz regime, as developed by the *científicos*, his ideologists, was a synthesis of ideas then in vogue in France, Britain, and Germany and rested firmly on the prestige which thinkers of these countries enjoyed among Hispanic intellectuals. What Díaz did was join Comte's conception of a progressive (but not demo-cratic) regime of technocrats to the post-Darwinian racial-ism that dominated historical thought at the time. This set of ideas implied that democracy not only was out of the question in the circumstances of Mexico since the Indian majority was clearly inferior biological material, but was in any case retrograde, since the best policies could be devised and implemented by economists and engineers guided only by the technical norms of their crafts.

It should be remembered that the revolution which over-threw Díaz initially took the form of a simple struggle for office. When Madero raised the standard of "effective suffrage; no reelection," he was pleading that office should be made available to a younger generation frustrated by the longevity of Díaz's *científicos*; at the time of the revolution, Díaz himself was over eighty, and his cabinet members were all in their sixties and seventies. The social goals which the Mexican Revolution came to represent attached themselves to its banners only after the fighting had broken out, and especially after Huerta's usurpation of office and the assassination of Madero, when the necessities of combat led to the widening of the scope of participation to new social groups, including the Indian masses. The generally socialist ideas that became the principles of the 1917 Con-stitution had thus not inspired the original revolution

directly, but they were undoubtedly "in the air" at the
time, just as the doctrines of positivism and racialism had
been "in the air" twenty-five years before. And the collapse
of the Porfirian political system was accompanied, even
preceded, by a collapse of the philosophical premises which
provided its ideological justification, as the Ateneo de la
Juventud, founded in 1909,[14] demonstrated when it
launched a program of reading and public lectures which
added up to a critique of the fundamental axioms of positivism.[15]

The Porfirian ideology, then, represented the adaptation
to Mexican conditions of the Comtean principles, then
fashionable in Europe and dominant in Latin America,[16]
summarized in the slogan "Order and Progress." This was
a deliberate reconciliation of the values of the Liberal and
Conservative forces that had contended for power in Western Europe and Latin America during the nineteenth century; the Conservatives, of course, stressing the need for
order, the Liberals rallying around the standard of progress.
The affirmation of the synthesis "order *and* progress," that
is, the rejection of the premise that the one excluded the
other, was especially well adapted to the needs of the
Liberal revolutionary who had come to power, such as
Porfirio Díaz: "progress," since he was a Liberal; "order,"
since he was president. It was similarly the logical slogan
for the Brazilian republicans, in opposition until the Empire was overthrown in 1890 and subsequently in power
for thirty years, and indeed "Order and Progress" was even
inscribed on the national flag of republican Brazil.

The stability achieved by many of the Latin American
countries during this period was of course buttressed by an
economic prosperity deriving from the prosperity of Western Europe, which implied both high demand for the
primary products that Latin America exported and large
capital surpluses that were available to invest in Latin
America. Political stability was underwritten by steady economic improvement, and the governments in power went
out of their way to create extremely favorable conditions
for foreign investment.

Economic well-being did not necessarily entail political

stability, however, as the example of Argentina demonstrates. Yet the Argentine case exhibits certain interesting similarities to that of Mexico. Again, it was a question of Liberals coming to power and synthesizing Conservative and Liberal policies; and again "order and progress" were tinged with racism.[17] In Mexico the Indians represented a large lower class population whose diligence provided the underpinning for the national economy. In Argentina, however, the Indians were hostile nomadic elements that were definitively subdued, either being killed or concentrated on reservations (as in the United States), during the period 1870–1879. The task development-minded Argentine administrations set themselves was thus not only to import European capital, which came to Argentina in vast quantities, especially from Great Britain, but also to populate the country with Western Europeans.

The creation of new social groups to which the immigration policy led, however, did not stabilize the new order, but rather created the conditions for the instability which has been chronic in Argentina since this period. Instead of populating the countryside and devoting themselves to agriculture, as had been hoped, the immigrants concentrated in the cities, especially in greater Buenos Aires, so that by the first decade of the twentieth century, the urban middle and working classes were composed predominantly of immigrants.[18] At the same time these classes were largely excluded from the political order since they did not qualify for citizenship and thus for voting rights. This enabled the old Argentine oligarchy to continue to dominate politics. At the same time, the food requirements of the larger population, together with the demands of industrializing Western Europe for Argentine meat and wheat, considerably strengthened the old land-based oligarchy, enriching it and reinforcing its identification with agriculture. Thus, the focal point of the Argentine oligarchy has been until today the Sociedad Rural, the interest group of the cattle owners.[19] The cleavage thus introduced between the rural Conservative oligarchy and urban elements led to a succession of participation crises and revolts centering around

the right of suffrage and the honesty of elections, which
were not resolved until the revision of electoral laws and
the holding of honest elections that took place under
Presidents Roque Sáenz Peña and Victorino de la Plaza.
The success of the immigrants in advancing themselves
socially and economically, however,[20] meant that when
European immigration was cut off during World War I,
a shortage of workers developed for Argentina's new light
industry, and an influx of workers of old Argentine stock
began from the countryside. This influx of rural Argentines
to the city remained slow as immigration revived after 1919,
but resumed with World War II, the yearly average rising
from approximately 8,000 before 1935 to 100,000 during
the war, and almost 200,000 between 1947 and 1951.[21] In
1936 12 percent of the population of metropolitan Buenos
Aires consisted of migrants from the interior; by 1957, it
was 36 percent.[22] These newly urbanized workers, ignored
by both the oligarch-controlled Conservative party and a
Radical party based on middle class sons of immigrants,
provided a reservoir of nationalist chauvinism and popu-
lism that was finally utilized by Juan Perón as his main
bastion in power. The magnitude of immigration from
Western Europe, its fluctuations, and its relation to
changes in social structure meant that economic development in Argentina led to political discontinuities and
participation crises as one group or another dominated the
system and to the injection of nationalist passions into
economic and social crises.

Thus the character and volume of foreign immigration
and domestic migration, responding to changes in international economic and political circumstances, helped
determine the structure of the informal sector of the polity
and the interests and ideological orientations of the participant groups. The significance of these factors appears
quite clearly if we contrast the case of Chile, which resembles Argentina in many ways, but which differed in
certain characteristics of its European immigration and in
its preexisting economic system and as a result was able to
develop a set of political dynamics more conducive to the

maintenance of constitutional norms. In the first place, although immigration to Chile was considerable, it was smaller than that to Argentina; around 1930, only about 2.46 percent of the Chilean population was of immigrant origin, and in the stratum of the population where immigrants were most heavily concentrated, the urban middle class, they formed only 17 percent.[23] This contrasts with a proportion of perhaps 65 percent in the corresponding stratum in Argentina. At the same time, the immigrant middle class entered a social system in which the relations between upper class and middle class were more fluid and could be described as interpenetration rather than cleavage and mutual opposition. The lack of dichotomization between upper and middle classes has often been remarked upon by students of Chilean history; it appears to have been due to a combination of circumstances, especially to the lack of a clear distinction between the economic interests of the two groups.

In the first place, the importance of mining and other extractive industries blurred the city/country distinction that was so crucial in Argentina. In the second place, the abolition of primogeniture and entail in 1857 made it possible for those whose wealth derived from trade and mining to buy land and thus become assimilated to the landed classes. It has been calculated that of the fifty-nine millionaires in Chile in 1882, the wealth of only twenty-four was based on land, that of the others deriving from mining, commerce, and industry.[24] Thus when the immigrants of the late nineteenth and early twentieth centuries arrived, a pattern of interpenetration between the middle classes and upper classes had already been established. The Conservative and Liberal parties, the former oriented to the landed interests, the latter to the cities, had frequently cooperated, and a pattern of excluding new social groups from participation had not been established.

A review of the cases just discussed suggests that a major factor in destabilizing a stable political order is a "participation crisis" induced by the exclusion of politically active groups from participation in the making of major decisions.

Most importantly, far-reaching destabilization of the political system appears to result from what might be termed a "participation crisis within a participation crisis," a situation in which a revolt against their exclusion from power by a relatively elite sector on the margins of the political system unwittingly brings about a more fundamental transformation of the political system as the process of revolt mobilizes lower class groups as well. Thus the attempt to be included in the political system of an excluded upper class or middle class group, such as the Maderistas in Mexico or the middle class Radicals of Argentina, may trigger a demand for participation on the part of more disadvantaged groups, such as the Peronist masses in Argentina or the Mexican Indians, just as the explosion of an atomic bomb is necessary to trigger the explosion of the hydrogen bomb of which it forms a part. This problem will be taken up again in the next chapter.

It was noted that the establishment of stable political orders toward the end of the nineteenth century was made possible not only by the ideological justifications which were available for them but also by the favorable economic circumstances of large capital imports from the Western European countries. No matter what actual contribution their acts of omission and commission may have made, governments are nevertheless held responsible by those who live under them for national economic conditions. In terms of the model constructed in the previous chapter, individuals and informal groups could accept the political order because they found both its ideological bases and its policy outputs congenial.

The breakdown of political systems under conditions of economic stress is of course well known in the history of Western Europe and has also been commonly found in the countries of Latin America; Charles W. Anderson has even coined the term "depression dictator," indicating the prevalence of the breakdown of constitutional forms under the impact of the Great Depression. Some evidence for the persistence in the post-World War II period of the tendency to political breakdown in the face of economic difficulty will also be given in Chapter Four.

In the terminology developed so far, it is clear that in the years since the breakdown of the stable orders that were achieved around the turn of the century, the political systems of Latin America either have been in process of evolution to a new stability in which social and political realities are based on the sets of ideas now accepted as legitimate, or else have been caught in the vicious oscillations of permanent instability as the tension between social and political realities and officially accepted ideas continues unresolved. It should be noted that these two states, evolution and permanent instability, need not be mutually exclusive and that evolution may in fact be taking place even though the statics of a system of permanent instability seems to obtain. This should perhaps be more exactly stated: A system may evolve toward a new stability by a dynamic process that resembles the fluctuations of a statics of permanent instability. This can be seen for Latin America as a whole during the years since the Depression, if one examines the relative incidence of dictatorships over time.

Has the number of dictatorships been increasing, decreasing, or remaining about the same? The answer given to this question depends on the starting point one chooses to take; economists have long been familiar with the problem of choosing the "base year." It has been pointed out earlier in the chapter that the special character of the period of political stability around the turn of the century has frequently been overlooked by observers, who have been brought to conceive of the twentieth century as a period of descent into increasing "instability and unconstitutional practice" by comparing the situation in some recent year with that in 1900.

It is equally plausible, however, to regard the stability of the turn of the century as exceptional and developments since that time as a reinvigoration of forces at work during the nineteenth century. That is, although evolutionary tendencies are at work, they coexist with traditional characteristics which produce a pattern of cyclical fluctuations. The complexity which this duality imposes on events has generally been misinterpreted, as observers have stressed either the cyclical or the evolutionary pattern to the exclusion of the other. Commentators have thus been either optimists, who perceive the evolutionary forces at work in the area as tending in a democratic direction, or cynics, who take an attitude of *"plus ça change . . ."* [25] The incidence of military dictatorships in the area seems to support the views first of one group, then of the other. A few years after Tad Szulc wrote *Twilight of the Tyrants*,[26] which

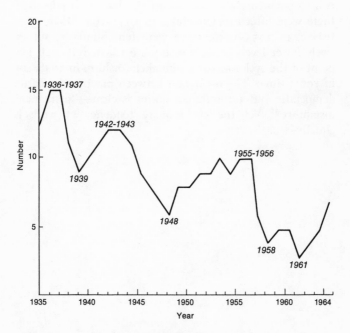

FIGURE 2. *Incidence of Dictatorship in Latin America, 1935–1964*

Numbers given refer to the number of unequivocally dictatorial governments in office for at least six months of the year.

celebrates the replacement of dictators by democratic regimes, Edwin Lieuwen can write a *Generals vs. Presidents*,[27] which analyzes the reverse phenomenon.

The relation of cyclical and evolutionary patterns on this point can best be demonstrated by a graph. Figure 2 plots the number of unequivocally dictatorial regimes in power during at least six months of each year, over the period of the last thirty years during which evolutionary changes have clearly been occurring.[28]

Conclusions of great interest can be drawn. Clearly, the factors which produce military dictatorships seem in part cyclical. At the same time, the cyclical pattern reproduces itself around a clearly descending trend line, so that each successive peak in the number of dictatorships existing contemporaneously is lower than the last: in 1936–1937, there were fifteen dictatorships; in 1942–1943, there were twelve; in 1955–1956, there were ten. Similarly, successively lower levels of dictatorship are reached at each low point of the cycle: in 1939, nine dictatorships; in 1948, six; in 1961, three. The oscillation between practices based on democratic and authoritarian norms is clear—"permanent instability." Yet the evolutionary tendency at work is equally clear.[29]

III
Violence

Three:
THE PURPOSES OF
VIOLENCE

If political stability is conceived of as the state of a polity which is functioning regularly in accordance with the norms it posits for itself, then the frequency of major outbreaks of political violence is related inversely to political stability. Accordingly, an analysis of the role played by violence in Latin American politics affords an avenue to the understanding of stability and change.

The prevalence of violence is of course one of the most characteristic features of politics in the area. While any general interpretation of Latin American politics thus involves dealing in some way with the problem of violence, there have been some explicit attempts to treat violence specifically and thoroughly. These have resulted in purely descriptive typologies of the modes of violence, constructed either by induction, as in the now classical article by William S. Stokes[1] or in Kalman H. Silvert's book *Conflict Society: Reaction and Revolution in Latin America*[2] or on the basis of some dimension postulated a priori, such as the scope or intensity of violence, as in the writer's *Latin American Politics in Perspective*.[3]

Most of the writing on the problem of violence in Latin

American politics, however, has properly consisted of attempts to understand and explain why politically significant violence occurs with such frequency. The major hypotheses proposed may be systematized under the following headings:

1. *"Racial" characteristics.* These long bore a major burden of explanation and Latin American writers still refer to them. The more sophisticated modern observers tend to ascribe to cultural heritage those characteristics formerly termed "racial." However, the "racial" approach can also be purged of its psychophysiological determinism to reappear in the form of a stress on social structure or modal personality;[4] we will return to this problem in Chapter Six.

2. *Cultural heritage.* The existence of a strong tendency to violence in Hispanic culture[5] has been so widely acknowledged that it is usually regarded as a directly observable phenomenon to be explained, rather than as a hypothesis that can be used to explain something else. Explanations of this heritage of violence often stress the fighting which took place intermittently over a period of seven and a half centuries in the Iberian peninsula between Moslems and Christians, only ending just prior to the time of the conquest of the New World.[6] Cecil Jane once[7] proposed a brilliant if tenuous explanation of the violence and political instability in the Hispanic tradition based on the formidable geographic barriers to communication and government activity in the Iberian peninsula. He argued that they led to isolation, regionalism, and strong desires for autonomy, on the one hand, and to the necessity for authoritarian government if anything was to be accomplished and political unity maintained, on the other. Jane found the key to political violence and instability in the resultant clash between extreme authoritarianism and extreme individualism.

3. *Geography.* Political violence has also been explained in terms of the geography of Latin America itself. One can distinguish three separate arguments here. The first stresses climate, especially the climate of the tropical and subtropical regions; the argument is that in a tropical climate man

is less capable of controlling his passions and in any case has less need to acquire habits of orderly work and disciplined behavior. Two other arguments based on geography are possible: that in small countries the seat of government is so accessible and the usurpation of power so simple that there is a greater temptation to attempt violent revolt; in the larger countries, it can also be argued, remoteness from the center, coupled with greater obstacles to communication, make it more difficult to maintain order and put down violence in the outlying regions.[8]

4. *Economic factors.* It is possible to regard the struggles between Conservatives and Liberals in nineteenth-century Latin America from a Marxist point of view with some plausibility, in terms of conflict between groups representing different modes of production. Insights can also be gained from a Marxist approach to political violence in the twentieth century, but the crude attempts to apply an exclusively Marxist analysis to contemporary Latin America have led to extraordinary distortions of reality.[9] A non-Marxist interpretation of instability and violence involving economic factors has been proposed by Merle Kling,[10] who has suggested that, since the control of wealth is static, due to limited entrepreneurship and other factors, the extralegal seizure of political power has necessarily become the major mode of achieving riches.

The author believes that insights into the problems of instability and violence are to be gained by trains of analysis starting out from each of these points of departure: race, cultural heritage, geography, and economic structure. Subsequent portions of the book will deal with some of these putative causal factors. In the present chapter, however, they will be regarded as givens, on the premise that violence does not occur with equal frequency in all countries of Hispanic culture, nor does it occur with equal frequency during different periods in the history of the same country, despite the fact that its geography and racial composition remain constant. It should also be recalled that the relatively high propensity to violence in the area as a whole is one aspect of the generalized failure to conform to constitutionally prescribed modes of behavior, due to their incompatibility with the realities of social structure, which has already been discussed. Yet deeper understanding of phenomenon of violence can be gained by examining in detail the various forms it takes.

The comments made in this chapter are based, therefore, on two distinctive premises: first, that the outbreak of *political* violence is on the whole a result of the workings of the political system; second, that "political violence" does not refer to a single type of behavior but to several different types of behavior, which perform different functions in the political system at different stages of its development.

Before classifying the different types of political violence, it should be made clear that such a classification may be used for analytic purposes but that actual instances of political violence do not necessarily fall completely into one category or another. It is useful to note the reasons why this is so. In the first place, there are borderline cases that combine characteristics of different types adjacent to each other on the spectrum. In the second place, different groups whose aims and interests are divergent may combine forces in a specific use of political violence, and the movement must then be regarded as a composite and not a pure type. In the third place, once the movement is launched it has its own logic. It responds to the tactical needs of the situation, to the nature of the resistance that it encounters, and to changes in the objectives of the initiators brought about by their experiences in the new situation. Even though difficulties may arise in typing any instance of violence, however, it is still necessary to approach empirical reality with a conceptual apparatus that can make it intelligible.

As a first stage in the classification of political violence we can divide instances into three categories: anomic, representational, and revolutionary.

Anomic Violence

Anomic violence can be regarded as violence which does not consciously aim at having an impact on the political system, although it may have political implications and effects. Its distinguishing feature, accordingly, is lack of coherent political purpose. Anomic violence thus performs functions primarily related to individual psychology rather than to the political system, such as releasing tension or providing an outlet for a desire to register a generalized protest against the world.

Representational Violence

In the model of the normally functioning stable polity, policy is the end product of a process involving what Almond and Coleman have called interest articulation and aggregation. Interests are articulated and aggregated by a series of structures which includes pressure groups, political parties, and legislative bodies. A notable characteristic of political processes in Latin America is the weakness of such intermediary structures.[11] A host of cultural, social, and institutional factors can be adduced to account for this lack of development of intermediary structures. I would like to stress two sets of explanatory factors. First, there are deeply engrained attitudes which assign individual importance on the basis of social standing. Such attitudes lead to a tendency on the part of ruling elites to ignore the wants of the masses, which reduces the role played by mechanisms for interest articulation; at the same time, they render the effective political public small enough so that contact can be maintained between it and governing personnel in the normal course of social interaction without the necessity for specifically structured channels of communication. Second, upper-class attitudes of aversion to systematic hard work and continuous attention to detail which undeniably exist mean that informal political organization is rudimentary, only intermittently active, and weak. These attitudes also render insignificant in effect the legally prescribed structures which could also serve representational and integrative functions, that is, the bureaucracy and the legislature.

The result is that statements of grievances and demands for their redress have to be brought directly to the attention of the president himself, since intermediary agencies are justifiably regarded as ineffectual. "Only the President can make a final decision. No other power is final, no other authority is absolute." [12] This necessity presents no problem for groups represented within the governing elite, which have regular informal access to the president. Interests outside elite circles, on the other hand, must resort to the public arena to bring their demands dramatically and forcefully to the president's attention. The events which took place in Ecuador during July 1962[13] illustrate this weakness of intermediary structures and the practice of nonelite groups to take direct action to bring grievances to the personal attention of the president if any redress is to be expected.

In July the Congress convened for its annual *sixty-day* session. In Machala local government workers struck to receive their back pay; the national government advanced the necessary funds to the municipality. Teachers in Pichincha province struck over the irregular payment of their salaries and a national strike of teachers took place in sympathy with their demands. "On the eve of the settlement hundreds of teachers and secondary-school students had assembled around the Plaza Independencia in the heart of Quito asking for the appearance of President Arosemena so that he could hear their complaints." Also in July the regional labor federation of Manabí province called a forty-eight-hour strike "to protest the lack of government interest in the social and economic problems of Manabí province. President Arosemena was asked to visit the province to view the situation himself. He declined giving as his reason a previously scheduled trip to the United States." However, the President did find time to fly to Guayaquil during July to arbitrate personally the conflict between the Banco de Descuento and its employees.

The common elements in all these incidents are the necessity to take direct action in order to secure the gratification of even the most patently legitimate demands, such as the payment of back salaries, and the need to secure the personal attention of the president.

The statement of grievances, moreover, must partake of the nature of a more or less veiled threat if it is to be effective. There are several reasons for this. The Latin American countries are faced today with very heavy demands for public services, deriving from the technical feasibility of new services, due to innovations in transportation, communication, and power generation; and a substantial and continuing increase in population, due at least in part to improvements in public health techniques. At the same time, a narrow tax base and inefficiency in tax collection mean that the gap between the demands made on government and government's ability to satisfy those demands progressively increases. Accordingly, it becomes of particular importance to have one's demands accorded a high priority if they are ever to be met. The threat of violence, or the staging of acts of symbolic violence, thus becomes a device not only to attract the attention of the president but also to guarantee that one's demands move up on the priority list and thus stand a chance of being acceded to.[14] One could then generalize that violence of the representational type is due to the lack of development of intermediary political structures, which in turn derives from cultural and social factors, and is intensified by the disparity between scarce public resources and the rising demands placed on them.

Revolutionary Violence

If one uses the term "revolutionary violence" in its broadest sense to distinguish it from violence of the representational and anomic types, this type of violence is distinguished by being directed at effecting a change of government. However, instances of revolutionary violence include a wide variety of types and must be distinguished on the basis of the scope of the change aimed at by the "revolutionary" group; the group may aim at changing personnel only, or policy, or structural characteristics of the political system itself. A key element of distinction here is the impact made by the revolution on the system of relations among classes—what has been called in previous chapters the system of social ordination.

A change in government brought about by extraconstitutional means without social class content or policy significance can be called, following S. E. Finer,[15] "*supplantive*," since the only purpose of its initiators is to supplant specific individuals in leading government positions. This type of "revolution," the revolving-door palace revolt clearly stereotyped as typical in the popular mind in countries outside Latin America, is no longer as common as it once was. Nevertheless, it still occurs on occasion, and it continues to serve only the purposes of personal ambition.

The "*good government" revolution*, on the other hand, may also be directed primarily against those holding office as individuals, but it is not designed to serve exclusively personal ends. This kind of revolution proposes to remove members of the government, and especially the president, because of alleged incompetence, corruption, or personal immorality. Although it is concerned with individual behavior, policy implications are nevertheless involved. Typically, military leaders who participate in a good government revolution are concerned not only with the censured behavior itself, but also with the effect it has on the nation's prestige abroad. At the same time, the alleged incompetence of the incumbent may provoke concern because it is thought of as weakness in the pursuit of a specific policy in which some group is especially interested. The belief that the government is unable to pursue some policy effectively may also shade into a suspicion that apparent inability is actually a protective mask for unwillingness.

Because of these concerns a good government revolution directed at first against the personal behavior of individuals in office readily develops into a *modernizing revolution* designed to reform outmoded or counterproductive features of the constitutional and administrative systems. Concern about the ineffectiveness or corruption of *one* incumbent government easily becomes transformed into a concern to make *any* government more effective and more honest by introducing structural changes. Such structural changes include revising legal codes, overhauling the rules governing the civil service, and reforming government organization and fiscal regulations. Again, the military may have a special interest in effecting a modernizing revolution because of the belief that the changes it brings about will result in an enhancement of national power.

In contrast to the types discussed above, the *democratizing revolution*, which is aimed at securing constitutional change that will admit groups at present excluded to participation in the polity, and the *socializing revolution*, which has as its goal change in the direction of greater equality in the distribution of the economic product, both have clear class content. The democratizing revolution leads readily to the socializing revolution, in accordance with the ancient maxim that the distribution of property tends to approximate the distribution of power. Accordingly, any attempt to change the distribution of power by admitting excluded groups to participation is correctly perceived by the possessing classes as a threat not only to their political position but to their economic position as well.

Each type of revolution that implies change more fundamental than a simple replacement of individuals by other individuals has as its counterpart a specific type of *counterrevolution*. The counterrevolution may occur after the fact or it may be preventive or preemptive, concerned to forestall a likely or even a merely possible seizure of power by those bent on introducing change, or the introduction of change by those already in power. Because of its defensive character and its preventive quality, the counterrevolution is less specific in its aims—that is, because of the tendency of one type of revolution to lead to another, it may be directed ostensibly against a modernizing or even a good government tendency, but is more fundamentally directed against the possibility that any change, no matter how small, may lead eventually to a socializing revolution. Because of this preventive character, the counterrevolution frequently seems to be directed against imaginary dangers, and its ideologists may seem to suffer from paranoid tendencies. Any suggestion of innovation, that is, may be regarded by counterrevolutionary leaders as opening the door to "communism," which is used as a negatively valued synonym for any kind of far-reaching structural change. Fear of communism and thus planning for the counterrevolution can be stimulated, accordingly, by the most minor and seemingly unrelated events.

Thus the counterrevolution is even more likely than the revolution itself to have a composite character, since those who collaborate in making it project a variety of negatively valued possibilities into the behavior of the incumbent regime.

A particularly natural and effective composite counterrevolution in recent years has been the seizure of power which combines the characteristics of a counterrevolution against democratizing and socializing tendencies with those of a revolution in favor of good government and modernization. Two recent examples of this type of combination are the Ecuadorean coup d'état of 1963 and the combined civilian-military revolt that took place in Brazil in 1964. In the case of Ecuador, the president who was overthrown, Carlos Julio Arosemena Monroy, was chronically under the influence of alcohol, and thus a natural target for a good government revolt. At the same time, the extremely archaic nature of the administrative, fiscal, and legal systems of Ecuador inevitably added a modernizing component to the revolt which overthrew him. These two elements coexisted in the revolutionary movement with a preventive counterrevolutionary tendency concerned with forestalling the democratizing and socializing possibilities inherent in some very minor and tentative steps taken by the Arosemena government. This counterrevolutionary tendency also presented itself, of course, as anticommunist, not only to the outside world, but also apparently to its leaders.[16]

This combination of aims also characterized the Brazilian revolution of 1964, which was directed against a weak, inconsistent, opportunistic, and corrupt president, João Goulart; but at least as important as these characteristics in marshaling the coalition against him were his democratizing tendencies, evidenced by his proposal to extend the suffrage to illiterates, and the socializing threat implicit in his land reform proposals.

This particular package of aims, which enables a counterrevolution to be presented as working in favor of good government, modernization, and anticommunism, has such a natural appeal that counterrevolutionary movements in general try to present themselves as being of this character. Thus the conspirators who overthrew Juan Bosch in 1963 routinely charged him not only with procommunism but also with corruption and administrative inefficiency, although his regime was at least as efficient and certainly a great deal less corrupt than any Dominican government has been since his overthrow.

After the success of a revolution which combines a modernizing and a counterrevolutionary tendency, a split soon arises between those genuinely interested in modernization, especially the military (who view it as a means to greater national power and prestige), and the oligarchic elements who had merely been using the military's desires for modernization as a vehicle to remove a government of progressive social orientation. This split does not take long to develop, because although some measures of modernization are socially neutral most of them impinge in some way on vested interests—certainly tax and landholding reforms do, but changes in legal codes and administrative regulations may have the same effect.

When this split occurs, the modernizing military find themselves on weak tactical ground. The process of modernization, especially as planned by military leaders, normally presupposes an authoritarian interlude during which the legal framework for the new administrative structures can be created and implemented by decree. This enables the counterrevolutionary representatives of the oligarchy to rally public support for their position that the military should now leave office and return the government to civilian hands. Their task is made even easier since the military government, unsure of itself and unskilled in the ways of civilian politics, typically resorts to excessively repressive measures toward the opposition. Thus the counterrevolutionary elements within the original revolutionary movement can now turn to the progressive opposition, by and large the very elements whose representative was removed from power by the original revolt, and create an "all-party" civilian opposition movement which soon results in the resignation of the frustrated and baffled military government leadership or in its agreement to hold elections.

It should be noted that the process described above is not the only way the forces representing modernization, counterrevolution, and social revolution may relate to each other. In the decade of the 1930s, and to some extent in the 1940s, the modernizing military more often made common cause with progressive forces to remove an oligarchic regime and then, shrinking back from the far-reaching reforms contemplated by their partners, made an about-face and concluded an alliance with the forces of counterrevolution. This was, in general, the path taken by the military in Bolivia and Venezuela during this period.

The distinctions made above are only one way of refining the concept of revolution so as to make it usable. There are other kinds of distinctions, valuable in other contexts, which can also be made. The classical distinction between the coup d'état, or "palace revolt," on the one hand, and the "real revolution" on the other, however, is not particularly fruitful in the present inquiry. The phenomenon known as the real revolution is characterized by a variety of features, and it is a strenuous but not necessarily a productive intellectual exercise to decide which of these features are the essential defining ones and which are not. For example, one can argue that the real revolution —that is, one which involves the restructuring of social reality—must be characterized by extensive violence. For a more detailed analysis of the whole range of processes of political change, however, in which the real revolution constitutes only one subtype, it is more helpful to examine the dynamics of the processes of change in each of their dimensions separately. For this purpose, the amount of actual violence that takes place is largely an accidental characteristic, and the process of fundamental social change may be brought about not only peacefully, but also gradually. In fact, if one wishes to talk about the "genuine revolution" and characterize it in terms of far-reaching and fundamental social change, it is quite clear that the authentic implementation of such change is necessarily a long and complex process, which normally *presupposes* the attainment of government power, rather than a violent struggle climaxed by the gaining of power. Thus the single critical element in the social revolution is the authoritative postulation of radically new goals for society, normally as the result of the coming to power of a new group.

Nevertheless, the assumption that a social revolution is more commonly violent than peaceful is well taken, even if the revolution is not over when state power is won, and even if the revolutionary group comes to power by peaceful means; for just as there are revolutionary ends a government may pursue, there are also revolutionary means it may employ. This point is discussed at greater length in Chapter Seven; we can say here that revolutionary means of government are those not in conformity with the preexisting "rules of the game"—that is, legislation by decree instead of by congressional enactment, seizures of property without compensation, and abrogation of the judicial process. Thus violence is likely to be a characteristic of the process of governing in a revolutionary way, just as much as of the extraconstitutional seizure of power. In both cases, violence, rather than reflecting the wishes of the revolutionary group, may be made necessary by the strength of the resistance to the changes contemplated, which varies with their scope. At the same time, prolonged violence in the struggle to attain power can itself have the effect of destroying the old society and establishing new social relations.

What is the basic motive force behind social revolutions, real revolutions, those described above as having a democratizing and socializing intent? Explanations of social revolution in terms of the single variable of oppression—the "worm turns" theory—can still be found, for example in this classic statement by Donald M. Dozer: "In general, revolutions may be said to result primarily from social pressures which have been building up for generations and which finally find an outlet in violent change." [17]

The analysis of major historical instances, especially that of the French Revolution, for example as generalized and summarized by Crane Brinton,[18] however, has surely made it clear that the crucial causal factor is not simply accumulated oppression but instead the frustration of newly aroused aspirations for change.[19] This view seems in addition to have a sound psychological base, since it is generally accepted that aggressive impulses derive from frustration. The point is that there is no reason to suppose that people who have been suffering for centuries will not continue to suffer indefinitely; only when they believe that change is possible but is prevented by the prevailing system from coming about will they take action to transform that system into another.

Analysis of the social revolutions that have occurred in Latin America during the twentieth century demonstrates clearly that they have been anything but spontaneous uprisings by the oppressed masses. The masses do not arise; they are aroused. An examination of the Latin American cases thus affords no evidence to support the "worm turns" theory but seems rather to confirm what Karl R. Popper has called "Plato's theory of revolution," [20] that there can be no successful revolution without a split in the ruling class or its defeat in foreign war.

The clear cases of successful social revolution in the twentieth century are those of Mexico, beginning in 1910, Bolivia, beginning in 1952, and Cuba, beginning in 1959; some observers would add to the list Perón's administration in Argentina (1945–1955) or the Acción Democrática governments in office since 1958 in Venezuela. The events in Guatemala beginning in 1946 constitute an example of social revolution which was brought to a halt (in 1954).

None of these cases represents the spontaneous uprising of an oppressed group. Spontaneous uprisings of the oppressed do occur, such as the land occupations carried out from time to time by Peruvian Indians; but they are ruthlessly put down by army and police as a matter of routine and are never anything but forlorn protests.

For the most recent of the social revolutions, that in Cuba, Theodore Draper has effectively refuted the thesis of an uprising of the workers and peasants in his *Castro's Revolution: Myths and Realities*.[21] A simple "worm turns" hypothesis could in any case never account for the occurrence of a social revolution in Cuba rather than in almost any other Latin American country, since in prerevolutionary Cuba the absolute level of per capita income was the third or fourth highest in all of Latin America, and the proportion of the national income going to wages and salaries in 1958 (rather than to profit, dividends, interest, and rent) was about 68 percent, apparently the second highest percentage in Latin America.[22]

In the Mexican and Bolivian cases, the social content which the revolutions came to have did indeed derive from the insistence of the demands of the oppressed masses themselves. The manner in which this came about is worthy of note, however. Normally, of course, the oppressed masses simply continue to remain oppressed indefinitely. They lack the self-assertiveness—what the authors of *The American Voter* call a sense of political efficacy and the authors of *The Civic Culture* refer to as subjective political competence—to take the sustained action necessary to reorder their social situation. The change in the masses' sense of political efficacy was clearly due, in both the Mexican and the Bolivian cases, to their being recruited to participate in combat; in Mexico to overthrow Victoriano Huerta, who had frustrated a simple good government revolution by removing Madero from office and having him assassinated, and in Bolivia to fight against Paraguay in the Chaco War.[23] Generalizing from these cases, one would then say that the social revolution does at least rest on broad support from the masses, even though they do not arise spontaneously when the accumulation of oppression passes their threshold of tolerance. The masses may have become mobilized by the experience of taking part in violence of another type; but they may also be mobilized consciously by the exhortation and organizational efforts of a leadership group capitalizing on the revolutionary possibilities afforded by the social situation. This leadership group may even have already come to power by means that did not suggest that a social revolution would be made.

The study of social revolution, accordingly, should not be limited to the more spectacular manifestations of violence, but must also be concerned with the strategies adopted by innovating government leadership. This problem is taken up in Chapter Seven, after the examination of some other questions which help to throw light on it. We turn next to a consideration of some empirical trends in the occurrence of revolutionary violence, in the broad sense, in the context of social change, giving special attention to the role of the military institution.

Four:
MILITARY INTERVENTION
AND SOCIAL CHANGE

A priori mutually contradictory theses about the relations of revolutionary violence to social development can be constructed—and indeed the literature on the subject abounds in such contradictory theses, evidence to support each of which is always available.[1] These hypotheses focus on whether revolutionary political violence, represented in Latin America most typically by the extraconstitutional seizure of power by the military, is (1) increasing or decreasing and (2) occurring primarily with the object of promoting socioeconomic change or of resisting it. Their starting points are the changes assumed to be going forward in the armed forces—the growth of professionalism, recruitment from a wider range of the population, greater influence from the United States, and so on.

Before proceeding, it is necessary to make two methodological points. First, if evidence can be cited on either side of a proposition about developmental tendencies, it is clearly necessary to quantify these items of evidence along a time dimension; what is needed, therefore, are empirical data giving the change in the frequencies of the occurrence of each of the contrasting possibilities over time. Second, if the approach taken in the previous chapter is correct, then the *frequency* of military intervention in politics is related primarily not to internal characteristics of the military forces but to the requirements of the functioning of the political system as a whole. The way in which a coup takes place, its structure and timing, can be affected by internal factors; and changes in the one can be expected to result in changes in the other. But the *occurrence* of a successful coup can be assumed to depend on what is happening in the larger political system.[2]

The empirical questions we want answered, therefore, are:

1. Since the breakdown of early-twentieth-century stability began the current period of change in Latin America, have extraconstitutional seizures of power become more or less frequent?
2. What changes have been occurring in the function of the coup in relation to changes taking place in the larger society?
3. What are the effects of changes in the Latin American military on the form, structure, and timing of the coup d'état, and what political significance do these effects have?

One must first eschew the hopeless task of trying to account for coups d'état that were not successful. The categories of coups that were aborted, suppressed, or abandoned melt into each other and into a host of other noncoup phenomena so as to defy accounting. At the same time, of course, since coups are after all illegal, they are matured under conditions of secrecy which make it inevitable that the unsuccessful projects for coups which become public represent a highly biased sample. At the same time, an unsuccessful coup attempt may be the work of one or two atypical people; its occurrence does not necessarily say anything about the state of the polity as a whole, as a successful coup does.

During the thirty-year period 1935–1964, there were fifty-six successful changes of government by extraconstitutional means in the twenty independent countries of Latin America.[3] The frequency of their occurrence was as shown in Table 1.

TABLE 1

Frequency of Successful Revolts in Latin America,
by Year, 1935–1964

1935	1	1945	2	1955	2
1936	3	1946	2	1956	2
1937	3	1947	1	1957	1
1938	0	1948	5	1958	1
1939	0	1949	3	1959	1
1940	0	1950	1	1960	1
1941	1	1951	2	1961	2
1942	0	1952	2	1962	2
1943	2	1953	1	1963	4
1944	6	1954	3	1964	2

Table 1 shows that the number of successful revolts normally fluctuates between one and three per year. The clearly exceptional years are those from 1938 to 1942, during which only a single coup took place. The first possible explanation is that these were years of recuperation from the Depression in which economic conditions were improving and the performance of government was likely to be regarded as satisfactory.[4] One would then hypothesize that a successful coup or revolt is less likely when economic conditions are improving.

A very rough test of this hypothesis can be made on the basis of figures for annual changes in real per capita product given in the U.N. *Statistical Yearbooks* for the 1947–1963 period. It should be borne in mind, here and at subsequent points, that statistical data from Latin America leave much to be desired. It should also be noted that the data are not complete. However, data are available, for most of the years during that period, for ten countries in which coups d'état occurred.

During 1947–1963, in those countries experiencing coups, real per capita income figures showed a rise over the previous year's figure eighty-seven times, a drop thirty-nine times, and remained the same ten times. (These figures cannot be assumed typical of Latin America as a whole, it should be noted, since it is precisely the countries whose economies are likely not to be improving which do not report reliable economic statistics.) If coups d'état occurred without relation to the state of the economy, one would then expect at least twice as many coups to occur in years which showed improvement as those which showed deterioration, since there were more than twice as many "improvement years" as "deterioration years." However, that is not the case. Of the fifteen coups occurring during years for which the economic data are available, seven took place during years which showed an improvement, seven during years of deterioration, and one when no change was reported. The incomplete nature of the evidence should be stressed; in future years more complete calculations will doubtless be possible; other factors, not now identifiable, may be partly responsible; but the available data are consistent with the hypothesis postulated, that the overthrow of a government is more likely when economic conditions worsen.[5] It should be noted that this conclusion was anticipated in the axiom postulated in Chapter One, that acceptance of a government is partially dependent on its satisfaction of popular needs.

It seems reasonable, accordingly, to regard the years of low coup activity from 1938 to 1942 as due to the economic recovery of that period. Since 1943, a very slight secular trend in the reduction of the frequency of coups is discernible. Since economic conditions are generally improving, although irregularly, this too might be expected on the basis of the same premise. Yet it should be remembered that variation in economic conditions can be held responsible for only a part of the variation in the frequency of coups, as the data discussed above also show.

We turn now to the question of changes in the function of the coup in relation to social and political change. This question is extremely awkward to get at, since the origins of coups are often obscure, the intentions of those staging them, mixed. The author nevertheless believes it sound to explain the coup functionally rather than genetically, in terms of factors external to the military rather than of internal characteristics of the military establishment, because of several considerations.

First, a military coup is not made by the military alone. Very frequently the conspirators are in touch with civilian politicians and respond to their advice, since they count on their assistance in justifying the coup to public opinion and in helping to run the country afterward. This relationship sometimes takes the form of a coup only reluctantly staged by the military at the insistence of civilian politicians, who appeal to the officers' patriotism, the historic role of the army in saving the country in its hour of need—of which national history doubtless affords many examples—and so on. As Víctor Alba puts it (perhaps too strongly), ". . . the militarist has no apparent objective apart from the immediate goal of power for power's sake; but, as often happens, he may be made the tool of certain social groups." [6] The chairman of one military junta which had outstayed its welcome spoke bitterly of some of its latter-day detractors "who used to cry at the doors of the barracks asking that the constitutional government be removed and even used to complain about the apathy of the military who did not want to act." [7]

Second, among the various conspirators, with their varying orientations and objectives, the position of those who can most count on outside support, whose own objectives are most in harmony with the aims of major outside forces, will be strengthened.

Third, the autonomy of the military decision to intervene may further be reduced by the fact that the political situation to which the military responds has been "engineered" by outside groups desiring intervention, so as to trigger military predispositions in that direction. It is not unknown, for example, for right-wing activists to fake "communist" terrorist attempts in order to help create an atmosphere conducive to military intervention.[8]

If the military coup is thus frequently called into play by the workings of the political system, what is its function in relation to social and economic change? Clearly, its purpose must increasingly be to thwart such change—because the point of the coup is to prevent from happening what, it is assumed, would happen in its absence.[9]

Since social mobilization is proceeding, that is, constitutional presidents are likely to be responsive to social classes of progressively lower status as these enter the political arena by moving to the city or otherwise become mobilized. The policies of each successive constitutional president are thus likely, on balance, to constitute a greater threat to the status quo than those of his predecessor. This may be interpreted to the military by those trying to secure their intervention as a threat to the personal economic interests of military officers, as a challenge to the military in its role of preserver of domestic order, as a threat to national unity and power, or as a long-term threat to the special status and privileges, even to the continued existence, of the military institution.[10]

It thus seems probable that as social and economic development take place:

1. Military intervention increasingly takes the form of an attempt by the possessing classes to maintain the status quo.
2. Military intervention is increasingly directed against legally elected presidents heading constitutional regimes.
3. Interventions increasingly occur to forestall the election and inauguration of reforming presidents.
4. Popular resistance to military intervention increases, resulting in greater likelihood that a military coup will lead to open fighting.

An analysis of the fifty-six successful insurrections[11] which occurred in the twenty countries of Latin America during the thirty-year period 1935–1964 appears to confirm each of these hypotheses and thus to substantiate the argument made above. Table 2 gives the numbers and

TABLE 2
Type of Successful Insurrection by Decades, 1935–1964

Type of Insurrection	1935–1944		1945–1954		1955–1964	
	NO.	%	NO.	%	NO.	%
1. Reformist	8	50	5	23	3	17
2. Low in violence	13	81	15	68	6	33
3. Overthrew constitutional governments	2	12	7	32	9	50
4. Around election time	2	12	7	32	10	56
Total	16	100	22	100	18	100

percentages of insurrections during each of the three decades of the period in the following categories:

1. The reformation of the social and economic status quo was clearly a goal of the conspiratorial group;[12] this shows a decrease.
2. A low level of violence (essentially a bloodless coup without street fighting or other popular involvement) was maintained; this also decreases.
3. Constitutional, rather than de facto, governments were overthrown; this shows an increase.
4. The insurrection occurred during the twelve months prior to a scheduled presidential election, or in the four months immediately following; this likewise increases.

Even if it be granted that the major determinants of the occurrence of a successful coup lie in the functioning of the total political system rather than in the internal dynamics of the military institution, those dynamics are of significance in such questions as the timing of the coup and become especially important in determining the directions followed after the coup is successful and its leaders are installed in government positions.

An examination of this problem must start from an appreciation of the fact that officers of the armed forces are not dominated by a single political viewpoint but hold a variety of political orientations. The correlates of these political orientations in personal characteristics have not as yet been systematically evaluated and weighed for the Latin American military along the lines of Morris Janowitz's *The Professional Soldier*.[13] Available evidence suggests, however, that on top of a primary set of conditioning factors such as those which the American voting studies indicate are the significant ones in party preference (family tradition, social and economic level, and ethnic or other particularistic identification) is imposed a second set of factors peculiar to the military profession: rank, branch of service, occupational specialty, and career pattern. In a situation in which a coup d'état becomes a possibility, ranking military officers are called on to develop policy positions on the question of the continuance in office of the president. The position each officer assumes will have two components, one based on attitudes toward the president's personal abilities, his programs, and the arrangements he is making for the succession; the other, partially independent of the first, reflecting the officer's views on the question of military intervention in politics in general.

The changes which have been taking place in Latin American armed forces in recent years suggest that the variety of political views represented within the military services has been on the increase, as the social origins from which officers are drawn have become less upper class,[14] as the range of military technical specialities has been extended, and as the sheer size of military establishments has increased.[15] At the same time, the increasing complexity of the governmental apparatus and the steady expansion of the proportion of the population which participates in politics, together with the technical improvement in the means of communication, have meant that a military coup needs itself to be more complex, to be more carefully planned, and to involve more people if it is to be successful. Because of heightened popular involvement in politics, a coup is also more likely to lead to open fighting, rather than being accepted passively by an indifferent population.

Given the range of political orientations within the military services, then, the task of the organizer of a successful coup d'état is to build up a coalition of officers of a size and character adequate to execute the successful coup. The prime mover or movers in organizing the coup must therefore be engaged over a period of time in the process of building a coalition which will eventually exceed, in size and "weight," [16] the minimum necessary to ensure success.

The originators of the conspiracy and the first to join it are those most opposed to the president and his policies,[17] while officers of different political orientations and a greater commitment to constitutional procedures have higher thresholds to interventionism. However, as time goes on, these thresholds will be reached for many officers as the tendency of the president's policies becomes clearer, as the country's situation, seen from their point of view, worsens, or as the succession problem becomes more acute with the approach of the end of the president's term.

It is possible that as time goes on the changes which take place in the situation reduce the degree of hostility to the president on the part of the organizers of the conspiracy, which may then disintegrate. It seems clear, however, that a successful coup would show a curve of support within the ranks of the military, rising over time and beginning with the original instigator of the plot, who represents the most extreme opposition to the president. The development of the curve of military support for the coup is likely to be exponential as the end of the president's term approaches. Under normal conditions the president prepares to hand over power to a successor of his own party or orientation, sometimes using not only his personal influence but also extralegal techniques to guarantee the succession. This raises the prospect of another four or six years of the same policies; the trepidation of those who oppose them necessarily increases. The heir apparent is in part an unknown quantity, which is disquieting; his previous public service will normally have taken place as a member of the president's cabinet, in which his own views necessarily had to be subordinated to those of his chief.

If there is a chance that the heir apparent would be defeated in the elections, the conspirators may await their outcome before striking. If he is indeed defeated, the need for conspiracy disappears; if he is elected, it then becomes necessary to strike before his inauguration, since his actual occupancy of the presidency would enable him to consolidate his power. Yet it is risky to wait until after the elections, which will mobilize his supporters and which may give him a strong mandate and thus strengthen his position with domestic and foreign opinion.

Thus, for these reasons also, the likelihood of a coup d'état could be expected to increase as a president's term wears on, reaching its high point prior to a scheduled election but remaining high until the inauguration of a new president, this tendency becoming more marked over time, in response not only to the accelerating social mobilization of the masses but also to the increases in the size, technical differentiation, and range of social origins of the officer corps.

Within the group of conspirators, then, a series of thresholds to interventionism is present. The lowest threshold is that of the instigator (or group of instigators) of the plot; the highest threshold, that of the last man (or group) to join in the coup before it was launched. The position of this hypothetical last adherent to the conspiracy is an interesting one to consider. If one recalls that the success of the coup is predicated on the formation of a decisive coalition to support it, then it is clear that the last adherent or set of adherents to the movement provided the critical margin of support, not just in its size, but especially in its "weight."

The importance of this hypothetical "swing man" in the situation may be due to any one of a series of factors —his personal influence within the armed forces; his prestige among the public; and/or his critical position in the command structure of the armed forces. It then becomes probable that because of his higher rank, greater prestige, and crucial importance for the coup, the swing man is placed at the head of the provisional government that emerges after the revolt is successful—as provisional president, as chairman of the ruling military junta, or as minister of the armed forces behind the façade of a civilian provisional government.[18]

An interesting and paradoxical situation is thus created. The swing man becomes the leading figure in the new government; yet he is the person who was least committed to the objectives of the coup, whose threshold to intervention was the highest of all the conspirators, and who was, as a last-minute addition to the conspiracy, perhaps out of sympathy with, or not even aware of, the more fundamental aims of the group that hatched the original plan. Indeed, a situation can actually be created in which the head of the new government never actually sympathized with the aims of the conspiracy, but joined it at the last minute only to avoid pitting brother officers against each other and possibly precipitating a civil war.

These characteristics of the swing man can be made clearer by an illustration. A classical occupant of the role of "swing man" has been Marshal Castelo Branco of Brazil. A *New York Times* reporter described his position in the 1964 coup as follows:

> General Humberto de Alencar Castelo Branco has been called a "general's general." He rose to his present post of Army Chief of Staff after a long professional career in which he gained the high respect of his fellow officers but remained virtually unknown to the general public . . .
>
> In the present crisis, the soft-spoken general first played the role of the reluctant dragon in refusing to join the developing movement against President João Goulart. His scruples were the same as those of many other Brazilian officers: The Brazilian Army has a tradition of protecting legality and the Constitution, and General Castelo Branco was not eager to become involved in a coup against a constitutional President.
>
> But the general became convinced that the continuation of the Goulart regime would lead Brazil to chaos and possibly a sharp shift toward the extreme left. He then drafted a position paper, the "Castelo Branco

analysis" that became the justification for the army's
support of last week's rebellion.

Such is the respect enjoyed by the short, stocky, bull-
necked general, that his analysis served as the turning
point in the hesitations of many commanders in the
crisis over Mr. Goulart.[19]

In this kind of situation ample material exists for a
conflict to emerge within the new provisional government.
The conflict develops along the following lines. The erst-
while swing man—now, let us say, president of the provisional junta—regards the objectives of the coup as real-
ized with the overthrow of the former president and
begins to make preparations to return the country to constitutional normality and to hold elections. The original
instigator of the coup and the group around him, on the
other hand, resist this tendency and instead urge the necessity for the military to keep power for a longer period, to
purge from public life all those who sympathized with the
deposed president, to outlaw his party indefinitely, and to
restructure political life to make it impossible for the
tendency which he represents ever to return to power.

During the recent period the basic situation described
above has been most faithfully reproduced in reality in
Argentina, Brazil, and Peru and with local variations in
Guatemala, Ecuador, the Dominican Republic, and Honduras.

In Argentina this basic set of dynamics has played itself
out again and again since the overthrow of Perón in 1955.
The irreconcilable anti-Péron forces are known as the
colorados, or "reds," and their most characteristic figure
is Admiral Isaac Rojas.[20]

Due to the more amorphous character of politics in
Brazil, the same basic situation crystallized more slowly.
The opposition between the military irreconcilables and
the heirs of Getúlio Vargas has nevertheless been waged
intermittently for ten years. The coup staged to prevent
the inauguration of Juscelino Kubitschek and João Goulart
in 1955 was unsuccessful; the coup designed to prevent
the inauguration of Goulart as president in 1961 succeeded

merely in curtailing temporarily the powers of the presidency; only with the overthrow of Goulart in 1964 was the military anti-Getulista movement fully successful. After the successful revolt of 1964, the pattern described above became operative in its purest form, with conflict developing between the prestigious swing man Marshal Castelo Branco, metamorphosed into provisional president, and the *linha dura*, the "hard line" of the irreconcilable military opposition to the heirs of Vargas.[21]

A similar process took place in Peru following the coup d'état of 1962. For thirty years the commanding officers of the armed forces had resisted the assumption of power by the revolutionary APRA movement, despite the fact that it commanded a majority, or at least a plurality, of the votes during the entire period. The party had begun in the 1920s and 1930s as a revolutionary Marxoid group, strongly anti-Yankee and prepared to use violence. During the thirty-odd years of its sojourn in the wilderness, however, the party leadership, and especially the party's founder, Víctor Raúl Haya de la Torre, had "evolved" to a more moderate position of which anticommunism was the central principle. At the same time, in a search for respectability which would allay the misgivings of the military about the party, the party's major tactician, Ramiro Prialé, led the party into alliance with increasingly more conservative forces, culminating shortly after the 1962 presidential election in an entente with the forces of General Manuel Odría. This was the ultimate stage of the party's evolution, since Odría was a former military dictator who had outlawed and persecuted the party during his period of office and who had run his election campaign in 1962 on a militantly anti-APRA platform. Haya had gathered more votes than any of the other candidates in the presidential elections of 1962, although only a handful more than Fernando Belaúnde and fewer than the one-third of the vote necessary to prevent the election's being decided by the congress. However, the new congress, due to the vagaries of the electoral system, heavily overrepresented the APRA. Immediately following the election, the coup was staged, the leaders of the armed forces implausibly charging that the electoral results were vitiated by widespread fraud. In an unsuccessful last-minute attempt to avert the coup, the APRA leadership announced that its congressional votes would go to General Odría in a self-sacrificing attempt to break the impasse and avert the breakdown of constitutional procedures.

This situation made possible the emergence of a more muted version of the split which occurred in the Argentine and Brazilian cases. The ranking officer of the military junta, General Ricardo Pérez Godoy, was willing to return the country to constitutionality on the basis of the APRA offer to have its congressmen vote for Odría. The two key younger members of the junta, Generals Lindley López and Vargas Prada, who had personal and family ties to Belaúnde, opposed this solution, which would enable the APRA to exact concessions, for example posts in an Odría administration. Pérez Godoy was accordingly forced to resign, and the reconstituted junta presided, during 1963, over elections in which, because of the withdrawal of two minor candidates, Belaúnde was successful.[22]

It appears overwhelmingly likely that as time goes on and popular participation in the processes of politics becomes greater, the Peruvian type of situation, in which over as long a period as necessary the popular choice is kept out of the presidency by repeated military intervention, will become increasingly common. As was suggested above, the pattern has already extended itself to Argentina and Brazil. Honduran politics seem to be moving in the same direction, as the army has become increasingly committed against the Liberal party; the Guatemalan military staged their coup in 1964 to prevent the return to power of Juan José Arévalo; and the Dominican armed forces have clearly attempted to assume a similar position relative to Juan Bosch and the Dominican Revolutionary party.

The logic of this type of situation suggests that the conflict between the most popular individual or party on the one hand and the military irreconcilables on the other tends to go on for some time, rather than being resolved by a single coup. This occurs for two reasons. In the military junta which forms after a coup, first of all, the irreconcilables normally are in a superior strategic position. The more moderate swing man, whose prestige has entitled him to the chairmanship of the junta, may wish to restore constitutional processes as soon as possible. If this is likely to lead to the coming to power of the individual or tendency originally vetoed by the coup, however, the position of the junta president becomes untenable. Although he occupies the position with most authority and he may have placed close associates in the cabinet, these are not the key posts under showdown conditions: the key posts belong to those in direct command of troops, that is, the minister of the armed forces, the three service commanders, and even the commanders in the field. Because of this lack of congruence between the positions of authority when affairs are moving smoothly and the positions of power when a split develops, it is frequently easier in such a situation to stage a coup d'état than to prevent one.[23] The odds are therefore that the irreconcilables will be able to prevent the return to constitutionality for an extended period if this should seem likely to favor the arch enemy.

Once military elements have vetoed the popular leader and his party, moreover, the hostility between the two becomes self-perpetuating and self-reinforcing, since those who participated in the original coup have reason to believe they will forfeit at least their careers, and perhaps more, if the outlawed party should ever gain power. As one Dominican colonel put it after the coup of 1963 when he was asked his attitude toward a return of Juan Bosch: "If Bosch ever comes back, he will throw me into jail so deep I will never find my way out." Because of this set of circumstances the restoration of constitutional procedures becomes extremely difficult; unless the distribution of voter sentiment changes drastically, it is only too likely that the person or party which secured a majority in the last election will do as well in the next one. A temporary return to constitutionality may be possible on the basis of rigged or restricted elections, as has been the case in Argentina. Nevertheless, the Argentine political problem was not permanently solved by such expedients, as the course of subsequent events showed.

Given the persistence of the military irreconcilables and their point of view, the only permanent resolution of the problem lies in (1) the definitive removal from the political scene of the vetoed leader by death or his renunciation of politics; (2) a shift of the distribution of popular opinion to the disadvantage of the vetoed party; or (3) the party's gaining respectability by drastic modification of its program or tactics. In Latin America, the third alternative seems only a formal possibility, since the irreconcilables may simply refuse to believe that the shift toward respectability is genuine. Thus the military veto against the APRA was still applied in 1962, despite the party's evolution to a moderate center or even right-of-center position. If the political problem has in fact been resolved in Peru—and this is not yet clear—it has been by way of the second alternative, in that the APRA may have been driven permanently below a third of the vote by a combination of disaffection from the left as the party's leadership has grown more conservative and the permanent establishment in popular favor of Belaúnde's Acción Popular. Elsewhere a similar result may be achieved, at least temporarily, by the expansion or contraction of the electorate to shift the balance of forces against the vetoed political movement—by giving the vote to resident aliens, for example, or by taking it away from illiterates.

This examination of the internal logic of the Latin American coup d'état in the circumstances of the current phase of history has so far led to three conclusions. First, the overthrow of a government is more likely when economic conditions are deteriorating. Second, as the military services have become larger and more various in the social origins of their officers, as military occupations have become more differentiated and more highly professionalized, and as elections have become representative of the sentiments of a wider range of the population, coups d'état have tended increasingly to occur in the period immediately prior to a presidential election and the subsequent inauguration, to be conservative in policy orientation, to be directed against constitutional governments,[24] and to be accompanied by violence. Third, the tendency has emerged for a conflict to develop, following a coup d'état, between a more fundamentalist "hard line" and a "soft line" that shows greater readiness to restore constitutional procedures and is normally represented by officers of higher rank, occupying positions of greater prestige in the provisional government.

It is possible to draw a further conclusion, with policy implications for the United States, from this analysis. There has long existed a difference of opinion among students of United States foreign policy as to both the desirability and the feasibility of attempting to discourage military seizures of power in Latin America. The desirability argument is outside our present province,[25] but it is possible for us now to add something on the feasibility question—that is, how successful the United States can be in attempts to discourage military coups d'état.

The failure of the United States to recognize a provisional government issuing from an extraconstitutional seizure of power, plus the imposition of other mild sanctions such as the suspension of military and economic aid, is of different effect to countries differently situated. The smaller countries whose economies are more dependent on actions of the United States—Bolivia, plus the countries of Central America and the Caribbean—are more susceptible to United States pressures than are the larger South American countries. Nevertheless, examples can be cited of military coups d'état which have taken place despite clear United States opposition, even in countries in the Caribbean area. These have been regarded as indicating that American opposition to such coups is ineffectual. The coup which took place in Peru in 1962 and the 1963 coups in

Honduras and the Dominican Republic, for example, took place in the face of strong and explicit American opposition.

It still seems premature to conclude that American opposition to the military seizure of power is bound to be ineffectual. One problem here is methodological, since it is not possible to enumerate the coups d'état that did *not* take place. If the analysis made above is correct, however, the success of a coup d'état depends, especially where the military services are large and highly differentiated, on adherence to the coup in its later stages of officers with least commitment to its goals, with less inclination to military intervention, and with more prestige and a higher position at stake. Since the success of the coup thus may well depend on its being joined by relatively few officers with a relatively weak commitment to its goals, it seems overwhelmingly likely that *any* deterrent to intervention —such as the suspension of military aid or a credible threat not to recognize the new government—while not sufficient to deter the hard-core organizers of the coup, may nevertheless be sufficient to tip the scales against intervention for the crucial swing man or for the small group occupying the same tactical position and thus may cause the coup to be abandoned or to be launched without adequate support and thus to prove abortive.

In the coup situation, accordingly, even the mildest deterrent threat, such as a firmly stated nonrecognition policy on the part of the United States, may still be effective, because of the structure of the pre-coup balance of forces.

IV
Economy, Society, Polity

Five:
POLITICAL DEVELOPMENT
AND SOCIAL AND
ECONOMIC DEVELOPMENT

One way of acquiring insight into the processes of political development in Latin America is to compare the countries of the area systematically in terms of the "degree of development" which each can be said to have attained. Ideally, such an enterprise can lead to the understanding of the past history of the "more developed" countries by reference to the present problems of the "less developed," while an understanding of the problems confronting the more developed countries can make possible a glimpse into the future of those now less developed. Isolation of the factors responsible for a state's being more or less developed can also prove instructive for the understanding of the relations between political and socioeconomic phenomena.

Perhaps most important, such comparisons provide the means for holding constant the effects attributable to characteristics shared by all, or nearly all, of the Latin American countries. It can be argued with much plausibility that military intervention in politics, say, derives from elements in the Hispanic tradition. Yet it is clear that the frequency of military intervention varies from country to country, even where they share equally in that tradition. Thus one is forced to go beyond the "Hispanic tradition" thesis with which the investigation might otherwise have come to rest.[1]

At the same time, a host of difficulties stand in the way of a fruitful classification of the Latin American countries by degree of development. Difficulties of major importance derive, as we shall see, from the problem of choosing which measurable dimension or combination of dimensions is most representative of the process of political, as distinct from social or economic, development. The aid that one can derive from the general systems of classification by either social or political criteria that have been developed is limited, since the Latin American countries tend to be concentrated in a limited number of the categories of those systems of classification designed to be world-wide in their comprehensiveness. For example, eighteen out of the twenty Latin American countries are embraced within only two out of the five categories of classification used by Bruce Russett, following Karl Deutsch.[2] All the countries of Latin America appear to be included in only one of the stages of political development proposed by A. F. K. Organski.[3] Accordingly, it makes more sense to think in terms of relative degree of development within the Latin American context, rather than on a global scale.

Attempts to categorize the Latin American countries by the stages of development which each has attained have highly varying results and of course are based on rather different conceptions of the process of development. It is nevertheless instructive to survey some recent attempts to establish an ordering of Latin American countries by their degree of *social* development that are based on essentially similar conceptions of "social development," that have been devised by thoughtful and sophisticated observers, and that are all based on relatively "hard" statistical data, primarily from the period 1950–1960.

Although the systems of rankings in Tables 3, 4, and 5

TABLE 3

Ratings on Social Development According to Almond
and Coleman (1960)

I	Chile, Uruguay
II	Argentina, Brazil, Costa Rica
III	Colombia, Panama, Ecuador, Mexico, Peru
IV	Bolivia

SOURCE: Gabriel Almond and James S. Coleman, *The Politics of the Developing Areas* (Princeton: Princeton University Press, 1960), p. 534. It should be noted that this "social development" ranking differs from another ordering made on purely economic criteria, in which Argentina is placed higher, and Costa Rica lower, than here. *Ibid.*, p. 541. It should also be noted that the ranking given here does not cover all the Latin American countries.

are based on similar conceptions and similar types of data and have partly similar results, the disparities among them suggest that the process of arriving at a composite summation of measurements in several dimensions allows considerable scope for variation.

One may summarize the common elements in these systems of categorization thus: Uruguay, Chile, Argentina, and Costa Rica stand out from the other countries at one end of the spectrum; Haiti, the Dominican Republic, and the Central American countries except for Costa Rica fairly clearly occupy the other end of the spectrum. The ten countries that occupy the middle ranges of the systems of classification prove more elusive to categorize, however; in Almond's and Coleman's view (Table 3), Brazil ranks

TABLE 4

Ratings on Social Development According to Germani
and Silvert (1961)

I	Chile, Uruguay, Argentina, Costa Rica
II	Mexico, Brazil
III	Cuba, Venezuela, Colombia
IV	Panama, Paraguay, Peru, Ecuador, El Salvador, Bolivia, Guatemala, Nicaragua, Dominican Republic, Honduras, Haiti

SOURCE: Gino Germani and Kalman H. Silvert, "Politics, Social Structure and Military Intervention in Latin America," *European Journal of Sociology*, 2 (1961), 62–81.

TABLE 5

Ratings on Social Development According to Labelle and Estrada (1963) *

I	Uruguay, Chile, Argentina
II	Costa Rica, Cuba, Venezuela, Panama
III	Brazil, Colombia, Ecuador, Mexico, Peru
IV	Bolivia, Paraguay
V	Guatemala, Nicaragua, El Salvador, Honduras, Dominican Republic, Haiti

* This typology is actually not original with Labelle and Estrada, and itself has an interesting history. According to the authors, it "is the work of the Center for Socioeconomic Development of Latin America (DESAL), an advisory and research body that works primarily for the German Bishops' fund for material development among the needy (MISEREROR). The DESAL 'typology' was done originally in spring 1963 for a critical report of the Alliance for Progress and has since been published in the Jesuit monthly *Mensaje* (No. 123—Oct. 1963); it is a considerable elaboration of a much briefer 'typology' done in Santiago de Chile in 1961 for UNESCO by Father Renato Poblete, S.J., and Father Roger Vekemans, S.J., both now on DESAL's board of directors." Yvan Labelle and Adriana Estrada, *Latin America in Maps, Charts, Tables*, CIF Study 1 (Cuernavaca: Center of Inter-Cultural Formation, 1963), p. 263. It is of interest that in a subsequent work Silvert has used a variant of this typology, rather than the one given in his 1961 joint article with Germani. Kalman H. Silvert, "Leadership Formation and Modernization in Latin America," *Journal of International Affairs*, 20 (1966), 318–331.
SOURCE: Yvan Labelle and Adriana Estrada, *Latin America in Maps, Charts, Tables*, CIF Study 1 (Cuernavaca: Center of Inter-Cultural Formation, 1963), pp. 263–267.

with Argentina and Costa Rica; according to Estrada and Labelle (Table 5) it occupies the same rank as Ecuador and Peru. Panama is placed by Labelle and Estrada in the same category as Costa Rica and ahead of Mexico and Brazil; to Germani and Silvert (Table 4), Panama belongs in the "least developed" category fully two categories *behind* Mexico and Brazil. Clearly the ranking of the Latin American states in terms of their social development, even where based on hard social data by competent observers, nevertheless includes a large element of subjectivity.[4]

The factor of subjectivity is also present when one turns to the question of the relationship between social and economic development on the one hand and political development on the other.

The case for the correlation of degree of stable democracy and degree of social and economic development has been made most notably in recent years by Seymour Martin Lipset.[5] In discussing the Latin American countries, Lipset shows that in indices of wealth, the countries he classifies as "democracies and unstable dictatorships" rate higher as a whole than those he calls "stable dictatorships." The indices of wealth he uses are approximately those regarded as indices of social and economic development by writers whose work has been considered above: that is, per capita income and the number of radios, telephones, newspapers, motor vehicles, and physicians per capita.

Although the present writer is convinced of the essential correctness of Lipset's point, as far as it goes, he finds Lipset's categorization of Latin American countries as either "democracies and unstable dictatorships" or "stable dictatorships" to be too idiosyncratic for him to accept Lipset's conclusions as they stand. Using Lipset's explicit criterion of "more or less free elections" over the forty-year period between 1920 and 1960, the present writer would have classed only six of the Latin American countries as stable dictatorships, rather than Lipset's thirteen. Three of the countries which Lipset classifies as stable dictatorships—Bolivia, Ecuador, and Panama—have actually at least as good a democratic record by that criterion as three of Lipset's democracies and unstable dictatorships— Argentina, Brazil, and Colombia.

The Almond and Coleman volume, *The Politics of Developing Areas,* also follows Lipset in showing a correlation, though one falling short of perfection, between economic development and democracy, the latter defined in terms of the degree of political competitiveness. The countries coded as "competitive" [6] were more likely to be found at the upper end of the economic ranking, those coded "authoritarian" tended to be at the lower end, and those considered "semicompetitive" were likely to be between the extremes. Although it would be utopian to expect perfect self-evidence in the categorization of countries by their degree of competitiveness, the author found himself unable to accept six of these twenty codings on their face;

moreover, in five of the six cases, the author's own use of the categories "competitive," "semicompetitive," and "authoritarian" would have given results tending to weaken the correlation between economic development and democracy. For example, for some time before the publication date of *The Politics of the Developing Areas*, the closest parallel to the Bolivian political system with respect to degree of competitiveness was to be found in Mexico. Yet Mexico—halfway up the economic ladder—is considered "semicompetitive" (which is not unfair, though debatable), while Bolivia, at the low end of the economic ladder, is labeled "authoritarian."

The correlation between economic levels and democracy, as defined by either Almond and Coleman or Lipset, thus appears to exist in much weaker form than either alleges. Before one can pronounce with assurance on the magnitude of the correlation, however, some way must be found to establish rankings or scores for democratic attainment that will eliminate arbitrariness and subjectivity.

In the attempt to eliminate at least individual subjectivity on this point, Russell Fitzgibbon has, over a period of twenty years, polled his colleagues in the field of Latin American studies to arrive at their conceptions of how democratic the countries of the area were relative to each other.[7] While Professor Fitzgibbon's rankings are not based exclusively on his own evaluations, they are of course still subjective. Moreover, he applies a complex and rather idiosyncratic process of weighting to the judgments of his panel. Professor Fitzgibbon asked his panel to rank the twenty Latin American countries on each of fifteen criteria that he has taken to relate to a country's standing as a democracy. The fifteen criteria are themselves rather imprecise, and it is a task of some difficulty to fill out the questionnaire. The major drawback in using the Fitzgibbon rankings as a basis on which to compare political with social or economic development, however,[8] is that some of the components of the evaluations requested from the respondents actually refer to social and economic, rather than strictly political, variables. Thus it may be that the evaluations on which the rankings by degree of democracy are based are contaminated by the inclusion of evaluations based on social and economic criteria.

It is accordingly not possible to accept at face value a correlation between the Fitzgibbon rankings and an economic development indicator, such as that pointed out by Charles Wolf, Jr.,[9] since the correlation can be suspected of being due, at least in part, to the economic component which entered into the political rankings themselves.

The problem thus remains that of finding a "hard" measure of stable democracy or at least stable constitutional functioning of the polity, a measure free from the implicit inclusion of social and economic evaluations and as free as possible from individual subjectivity.

An interesting attempt in this direction has been made by Phillips Cutright in an article entitled "National Political Development: Its Measurement and Social Correlates."[10] Cutright constructed an index of political development (understood in a democratic sense) based on such acknowledged criteria of democracy as freedom of elections and respect for their results, and the existence and size of opposition representation in the legislature. The index was formed by assigning to each country one point for every year in which it was ruled by a chief executive chosen in free elections, one point for every year in which more than one party was represented in the legislature, and one point for every year in which a minority party held more than 30 percent of the legislative seats.

This represents a substantial contribution in some respects. Using the year as a unit of measurement creates the possibility of plotting positions along a dimension which has a more than purely notional meaning. Moreover, assigning one point for each year in which a chief executive chosen in free elections actually *remained* in office reflects not only the number of free elections that were held, à la Lipset, but also the degree of respect for their results which existed; this is an important variable in the Latin American context. However, taking the existence of a legislative opposition into account in constructing the index drastically distorts the results obtained. This is so, among other reasons, because it is common practice in Latin America to provide for the mandatory representation of opposition parties in the legislature. During the period following the end of World War I used by Cutright, at least six Latin American countries operated under constitutional or legal provisions earmarking legislative seats for an opposition party. The irony of the situation, and the reason that use of this criterion distorts Cutright's index so greatly, is that the provision for guaranteed opposition representation is particularly favored by the dictatorships, because it serves to give foreign democrats the illusion of a tolerated opposition. The opposition members, however, even if they hold the up-to-33 percent of the legislative seats legally guaranteed them, are of course powerless to oppose legislation passed by a disciplined majority loyal to the president. It is generally recognized that, under these conditions, provisions for guaranteed legislative seats for the opposition constitute no more than democratic window dressing, and legitimate democratic opposition parties normally boycott elections that they feel will be conducted so as to favor the president's party. At the same time, however, there is never a lack of opportunists, sometimes renegades from the democratic opposition, who will organize a spurious opposition party to contest the elections in order to enjoy the privileges and emoluments of the opposition legislative seats, which are really sinecures.

The distortion introduced by considering the existence of a formal legislative opposition as a factor in determining a country's political development can be seen in the case of Nicaragua. During most of the period covered by Cutright's article, Nicaragua was a notorious dictatorship under the Somoza family, easily one of the two or three most stable dictatorships in Latin America. And yet on Cutright's scale of political development, which embraces all the independent countries in the world, Nicaragua scores the same number of points as the Netherlands—substantially more than Israel or Austria—and enjoys the fifth highest place among the Latin American countries.

The difficulties encountered by Cutright may be drastically reduced, however, if a noncomposite index is constructed, based solely on the number of years a country has been ruled constitutionally. A "constitutional" year can be operationally defined as one in at least six months of which the country was ruled by a government chosen in (more or less) free elections *and* in which that government on the whole respected constitutional procedures and individual civil liberties *and* in which no extraconstitutional changes of government took place. This captures the two aspects of a government's democratic legitimacy, its origin and its performance, in a more reliable way than Cutright's index.

Table 6 gives, in Column 1, the number of years during

TABLE 6
Years of Constitutional Government, 1935–1964

Country	1 STRICTLY DEFINED	2 LOOSELY DEFINED	3 MEAN OF 1 AND 2	4 RANK ORDER BASED ON 3
Chile	30	30	30.0	1
Uruguay	27	27	27.0	2
Costa Rica	24	30	27.0	2
Mexico	24	30	27.0	2
Panama	20	29	24.5	5
Colombia	20	22	21.0	6
Brazil	16	19	17.5	7
Ecuador	13	22	17.5	7
Bolivia	11	18	14.5	9
Peru	9	18	13.5	10
Guatemala	10	14	12.0	11
Cuba	8	15	11.5	12
Honduras	5	14	9.5	13
Argentina	4	13	8.5	14
Venezuela	6	9	7.5	15
El Salvador	0	13	6.5	16
Nicaragua	1	9	5.0	17
Paraguay	1	4	2.5	18
Dominican Republic	0	4	2.0	19
Haiti	0	1	0.5	20

SOURCE: The data were compiled, from a variety of sources, by Walter C. Soderlund, and classified by Mr. Soderlund and the author.

the period from 1935 to 1964 inclusive (approximately the length of time in which democratic practices have begun to take hold widely in Latin America) which qualified as "constitutional and democratic" years on the basis of the criteria stipulated above. Clearly, coding problems arise here, and there are a great many borderline cases. To take this into account, Column 2 gives the number of years not spent under governments which were unequivocally dictatorial; that is, it includes, in addition to the years totaled in Column 1, years spent under provisional governments and under other governments not democratically elected which nevertheless ruled constitutionally. Column 1 thus reflects exacting, Column 2 permissive, criteria of constitutionality. Column 3 gives the means between the two sets of figures, thus providing an index of constitutionality that is rough but one that is probably as authentic as any that can be devised. The rank ordering in Column 4 is based on the mean figures of Column 3.

If we return to the question of the correlation of degree of stable democracy with level of economic well-being, now on the basis of rather "harder" data, some relation, but a rather weak one, is found to exist. The coefficient of correlation between the constitutionality index figures of Column 3 and life expectancy at birth (which, following Russett,[11] can be regarded as a naturally "composite" index of socioeconomic well-being) is 0.37.

Figure 3, which is a "scattergram" plotting rank order on the constitutionality index against that on gross national product per capita,[12] indicates these relations graphically. The hypothesis that political development correlates with economic development can be regarded as being weakly confirmed, in the sense that the top right and bottom left quadrants are fuller than those at top left and bottom right. Deviations from the center line appear greater than would be expected in terms of the Lipset or Almond and Coleman theses. If one thinks in terms of an undifferentiated process of socioeconomic development, or "social mobilization," of which gross national product per capita is simply one indicator,[13] then clearly social

mobilization stands in some causal relation to political development (defined as the attainment of stable constitutional functioning), but is modified by, or mediated
through, other characteristics of the social system that
make its effects not wholly determining.

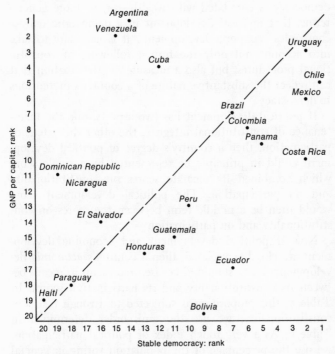

FIGURE 3. *Wealth and Stable Democracy*

Broken line indicates positions that would be occupied if the two characteristics were perfectly correlated.

But this result was only to be expected; the attainment
of stable constitutional functioning is, after all, only the
formal dimension in which political development takes
place. As was pointed out in the Introduction, to specify
adequately the concept of political development for our
era, one also has to stipulate the substantive dimension,

which is the extent of participation in the polity on terms of equality.

Thus the attainment of constitutional stability can be regarded as only one aspect of political development, the other being extent of participation. If one wishes to perform a more adequate test of the proposition that stable democracy is correlated with wealth—or, in more general terms, that political development in a democratic era accompanies economic development—it is necessary to take into account not only the formal following of constitutional procedures, but also a measure of participation that can reflect the substantive nature of a country's pretensions to democracy.

If political development has two aspects, one the maintenance of constitutional integrity, the other the extent of participation, then a country's degree of political development could in principle be represented by a single score which combined its separate scores on constitutionality and on participation. The political development score would then be a middle term between the scores on constitutionality and on participation.

Now if political development and economic development are closely correlated, then a country's *economic* development score should, likewise, represent a mean between its constitutionality and its participation scores. In Table 7, this proposition is subjected to a rough test. For constitutionality, we use the rank order determined in Table 6. As a very rough index of political participation, we use the percentage of the population voting in general elections around 1960, using figures referring to relatively fair elections where available. These electoral participation figures are not wholly satisfactory for several reasons. Apart from the point that electoral participation is only roughly related to political participation in general, it is clear that electoral participation may be affected by transitory circumstances peculiar only to the election in question and not reflecting long-term regularities. At the same time a slight bias probably exists in the participation figures due to the difference in age distribution from country to country. In other words, some countries—especially those with lower birth rates: Argentina, Uruguay, and Paraguay—have a larger proportion of the population over the minimum voting age than others, quite apart from the variations in the rules governing voters' eligibility. It is also true that the freest elections for which figures are available were sometimes not very free. The figure for Cuba is especially unsatisfactory on this score. Cuba has not had a free election for twenty years, and a good case could be made for leaving Cuba out of the reckoning entirely; but instead the figure for the less-than-free presidential election of 1954 has been used. Accordingly, what follows should be regarded as no more than a provisional statement until further refinement is made possible by the availability of more and better data and the application of more sophisticated techniques than those at the author's command.

If the hypothesis we are testing is correct, the indicator of economic development (again, life expectancy) should appear as a mean term between the constitutionality indicator and the participation indicator. If the hypothesis is incorrect, then the economic development indicator should appear as a mean term in slightly less than one-third of the cases, that is, about six times out of twenty. Table 7 gives the rank orders for the twenty Latin American countries with respect to the three indicators.[14]

As Table 7 shows, the hypothesis is confirmed in thirteen of the twenty cases, or about twice the frequency that one could expect if the relationship hypothesized did not hold.[15] Of course, this remains a relatively crude test.

Stronger confirmation of the hypothesis is provided, however, by computation of coefficients of correlation among the three sets of raw scores. The correlation between the economic development indicator (life expectancy) on the one hand and the political development indicators (the constitutionality index and electoral participation figures) on the other, is 0.69, which is significant at the 0.01 level. If per capita gross national product (Russett's figures) is substituted for life expectancy as the indicator of economic level, the correlation actually rises to 0.72. The significance

TABLE 7

Comparison of Rank Orderings on Constitutionality, Economic Development, and Participation

Country	CONSTITUTIONALITY	ECONOMIC DEVELOPMENT (LIFE EXPECTANCY)	ELECTORAL PARTICIPATION
Argentina	14	2	1
Bolivia	9	20	8
Brazil	7	8	14
Chile	1	7	15
Colombia	6	13	17
Costa Rica	2	3	6
Cuba	12	3	10
Dominican Republic	19	16	4
Ecuador	7	17	18
El Salvador	16	14	16
Guatemala	11	18	19
Haiti	20	19	7
Honduras	13	15	13
Mexico	2	10	11
Nicaragua	17	11	5
Panama	5	5	11
Paraguay	18	8	10
Peru	10	12	20
Uruguay	2	1	3
Venezuela	15	6	2

SOURCE: Constitutionality index, see Table 6; life expectancy, Bruce Russett, *et al.*, *World Handbook of Political and Social Indicators* (New Haven, Conn.: Yale University Press, 1964), pp. 197–198; electoral participation, Yvan Labelle and Adriana Estrada, *Latin America in Maps, Charts, Tables*, CIF Study 1 (Cuernavaca: Center of Inter-Cultural Formation, 1963), p. 230, except for figures on Cuba, Nicaragua, Paraguay, and the Dominican Republic, which are calculated by the author from population figures given by Russett, *op. cit.*, pp. 18–20, and election results given in the *Hispanic American Report* for February 1963 (Dominican Republic) and April 1963 (Nicaragua and Paraguay). The figure for Cuba is from the *Statistical Abstract for Latin America, 1956* (Berkeley and Los Angeles: University of California Press, 1957).

level of 0.01, again, means that the chance of this outcome's having occurred if the variables were not correlated is no more than one in a hundred.

The necessity of taking both aspects of political development into account is demonstrated by the smaller size of the correlation of the economic development indicator with the indicators of either aspect of political development alone. The correlation of life expectancy with the constitutionality score is 0.37, significant at the 0.1 level, and with the electoral participation figure is 0.49, significant at the 0.05 level.

It can be stated with a considerable degree of assurance, therefore, that political development, conceived of as the heightening of *both* observance of constitutional norms *and* popular participation in politics, is indeed commensurate with economic development.[16] This has not appeared clearly in the literature so far because, among other things, authors have relied on conceptions of political development which stress either the constitutional stability factor or the participation factor but not both.

One interesting aspect of the relationships described above is that—for the intermediate stages of political development, at least; that is, before the attainment of completely stable functioning and maximum participation—there is a partially *inverse* relation between stability and participation.[17] In other words, a country that develops economically develops politically, but this heightened level of political development can appear either as a greater fidelity to constitutional norms or as a higher degree of participation in political processes; whether one or the other direction is taken depends apparently in large part on the degree of egalitarianism in the social structure, the causes for which will be discussed in the next chapter.

This formulation appears to confirm the scattered impressionistic insights of previous observers; for example, it can be regarded as an alternative formulation of Bagehot's principle, reemphasized in recent years by Harry Eckstein, that the stability of the British constitutional order has been due to the deference showed by the British lower class to its social superiors. The deference premise is equivalent to saying that, economic levels remaining constant, constitutional stability increases in proportion to social inequality, or in proportion to the degree possible participants refrain from active political participation.[18]

One might also transpose the argument into the following terms: any stable political order needs to embody the principle of authority and, to some extent, that of hierarchy. In a democratic political order, however, these principles necessarily conflict with the principle of equality. As one reaches higher levels of economic and social development, however, the resources are created which enable a society embodying both types of principle to survive—resources, that is, of private satisfactions, of governmental budgetary capability, and of education and political sophistication.

Conclusions of interest can be drawn by contemplating the implications of change in the various components of this set of relationships.[19] If participation is treated as the independent variable, then if participation increases greatly, constitutional integrity will tend to deteriorate unless the country's economy develops at the same time, providing a higher level of welfare to match the higher level of participation.

Chile provides a recent case of the working out of this set of relationships in Latin America. Constitutional stability in Chile has always been high—in the Latin American context—except for an interlude during the Depression. Chile's economic level has been relatively rather low, however, and, as the theory outlined above would predict, participation has also been extremely low; the turnout of 17.9 percent of the population in the presidential election of 1958 represents the high point reached by electoral participation to that time. Politicization advanced, however, as Christian Democrats and the Socialist-Communist alliance, FRAP, competed in organizing the masses, even including the hitherto neglected rural population. Thus electoral participation rose to 26.76 percent of the population for the 1963 municipal elections and finally to 31.82 percent for the climactic presidential election of 1964.[20] It was generally thought that this election was crucial for deciding whether Chile's future path would be democratic or not. With the victory of the Christian Democratic candidate, the probability grew that Chile could make the "breakthrough" into a political order that would allow for both constitutional stability and high participation, on the Uruguayan pattern—that is, a political order in which democracy could be strong both formally and substantively. The Christian Democratic government moved in the direction of fulfilling its historical task by attempting to remove the last barriers to total participation by abolishing the literacy requirement for voting and organizing peasant unions. At the time of writing the reform had not been consummated, although the odds were in its favor. Clearly, however, the new political order could only persist if it were underpinned by the higher level of economic well-being that would be demanded by the newly participant groups, who would be likely otherwise to reject the established system and turn to anticonstitutional alternatives. This was clearly understood by the Christian Democratic administration, whose "revolution in liberty" aimed at the maintenance of constitutional norms while reaching new heights not only of participation and equality, but also of production and welfare.

On the other hand, a high order of constitutional integrity can be maintained while economic conditions are deteriorating only by politically restrictive policies which lead to a reduction in participation. This is demonstrated by developments in Colombia under the presidency of Guillermo León Valencia (1962–1966); constitutional stability was guaranteed by the bipartisan National Front agreement, the economy stagnated, and the already low electoral participation showed a drop. If participation in Colombia increases substantially, therefore, constitutional stability can only be maintained by a resumption of economic growth.

Some superficially paradoxical but extremely interesting conclusions for the understanding of dictatorship also follow. A low order of constitutional integrity, that is, a state of anarchy or dictatorship, is compatible with a low order of political participation only where the degree of social and economic development is also low. For higher levels of economic development, however, the imposition of dictatorship should tend to increase "participation." This apparent paradox can be understood in the sense that under a dictatorship aspects of life which were formerly not politicized become so, and individuals previously apathetic toward politics need to start paying attention to political factors.

The politicization of the population of an economically developing country by a dictatorship has effects which surprise outside observers. One of these is the "unexpectedly" high electoral participation in the free elections held after the overthrow of the dictator; the extremely high turnout figures in Venezuela after Pérez Jiménez and in the Dominican Republic after Trujillo are well known. Similarly, parties whose success depends on the politicization of marginal members of the society, such as the Communist and other extremist parties, typically do much better after the overthrow of the dictator than they did before his assumption of power. Thus the vaunted "stability" provided by dictatorship is almost invariably the prelude to extreme turbulence.[21] It should also be pointed out that in a fairly well developed society the dictatorship itself finds that it has to encourage mass participation in its own subsidiary organs in order to maintain itself in power. This is what is meant by the frequently made observation that in a developed society a dictatorship tends either to be overthrown or to become totalitarian.[22]

We are now in a position to see what was wrong with the standard formulations, of which Lipset's is the best known, which correlate "stable democracy" and "wealth." Stable democracy, or "political development," is usually defined solely in terms of the observance of constitutional norms—but this is a purely formal criterion which does not take into account the difference between countries where constitutional forms are a façade masking an undemocratic reality and those in which observance of constitutional forms is accompanied by general political participation and a democratic spirit.

It is understandable that those especially concerned with social justice in Latin America should become impatient with traditional formulations of this type and, conscious of the realities of social inequality that lie behind the constitutional façade, become cynical about constitutional forms and espouse revolutionary ideology.

The problem is a genuine one. At any level of development between the extremes of the completely underdeveloped and the completely developed societies (the latter represented in Latin America, if at all, only by Uruguay) there is an inverse relationship between mass participation and constitutional stability.[23] One is thus presented with a dialectical tension: if mass participation rises faster than the level of economic development, then constitutional functioning breaks down, usually with the imposition of a military regime, as conservative forces in the society react against the attempts of constitutional governments to gratify desires of the newly participant masses through drastic social change. This conclusion was in fact indicated by the data on coups d'état given in Chapter Four.

It is thus possible to explain on the basis of the foregoing principles some of the apparent failures of the hypothesis that stable democracy and wealth are correlated. Three of the wealthiest countries in Latin America by gross national product per capita figures—Argentina, Cuba, and Venezuela—have at the same time extremely poor records of constitutional integrity. The point is shown clearly by the scattergram in Figure 3. This is not surprising in view of the formulation developed here, that for any intermediate level of development there is an inverse relation between mass participation and constitutional stability, since these three countries have extremely high orders of mass participation. This cannot be shown in terms of electoral participation for Cuba since there have been no free Cuban elections recently, but Argentina and Venezuela rank first and second respectively in electoral turnout, as Table 7 shows. The high order of participation in all three is suggested by the figures on the proportion of the population unionized (Table 8); in 1960 over 10 percent of the population was unionized in each of these three countries (even though union membership dropped over 50 percent

TABLE 8

Labor Organization Membership, 1960

Country	UNION MEMBERSHIP (1,000s)	TOTAL POPULATION (1,000s)	PERCENTAGE
Argentina	2,576	20,998	12.2
Bolivia	200	3,709	5.4
Brazil	2,500	65,862	3.8
Chile	493	7,634	6.5
Colombia	330	14,771	2.2
Costa Rica	23	1,114	2.1
Cuba	1,504	6,797	22.0
Dominican Republic	188	2,845	6.6
Ecuador	85	4,287	2.0
El Salvador	36	2,396	1.5
Guatemala	16	3,755	0.4
Haiti	10	3,726	0.3
Honduras	18	1,932	0.9
Mexico	2,101	34,626	6.1
Nicaragua	16	1,465	1.1
Panama	15	1,052	1.4
Paraguay	20	1,624	1.2
Peru	550	10,857	5.1
Uruguay	197	2,760	7.1
Venezuela	1,500	6,933	21.6

SOURCE: For union membership, United States Department of Labor, *Directory of Labor Organizations, Western Hemisphere,* United States Department of Labor (Washington, D. C.: Government Printing Office, 1960), Vol. I, pp. xii–xiii; for population, Ivan Labelle and Adriana Estrada, *Latin America in Maps, Charts, Tables,* CIF Study 1 (Cuernavaca: Center of Inter-Cultural Formation, 1963), p. 62, except for the misprinted Cuban figure, which is substituted for by the figure given for Cuba (midyear, 1960) in the *Statistical Abstract of Latin America, 1965,* 9th ed. (Los Angeles: University of California Press, 1966), p. 14.

in Argentina after the overthrow of Perón), but this was true in no other country in Latin America. It is also in Argentina and Cuba that dictatorship has most shown the characteristics of twentieth-century totalitarianism, and Venezuela probably has come as close as any other country in the area to following the Cuban path.

It has been suggested in this chapter that the chief determinant of whether political development became expressed in higher levels of constitutional stability or in increased political participation was the degree of equality in a country's social structure, the more hierarchic countries becoming more stable, the more egalitarian countries becoming more participant. We turn next to the question of social equality, which in Latin America is bound up with the question of race.

Six:
SOCIAL STRUCTURE, "RACE,"
AND POLITICS

It is understandable that the category of race, which bore the major brunt of social explanation in discussions of Latin America seventy years ago, should almost have disappeared as an explanatory tool. The twentieth century has taught us to beware of racial explanations of social phenomena. Perhaps, however, an opportunity has been missed to use the category of race not as an intrinsic factor in explaining individual behavior but, in the Latin American context, as a crude but efficient indicator of social structure. For example, one may use the fact that Peru is a heavily Indian country not to explain political behavior in Peru by reference to putative behavioral characteristics of a Peruvian Indian race, which would in any case be foolish, since the effective political class in Peru is clearly not composed of Indians, but rather to indicate that, because of the identification of social distinctions with those of race common in Latin America, the presence of a large number of Indians in Peru means that Peruvian social structure is of a certain kind, which imposes certain characteristic patterns on Peruvian politics.

It should be understood that in this context the concept of race is not biological, or only biological in its remote origins, but is primarily social, as Charles Wagley has suggested by the concept of "social race." [1] Thus social structure and the concept of race have modified each other reciprocally with the result that, while in several countries social structure is basically defined in "racial" terms, the concept of race itself has reference to sociocultural, rather than biological, realities.[2] Of course, in many preindustrial polyethnic societies social status and occupation are ethnically determined, and this also occurs in some nonindustrial sectors of industrial societies; but in Latin America, in addition, "racial" identification is itself partly a function of class and occupation.

If one thinks in historical terms, it is quite clear why this should be so, for the racial composition of the Latin American societies was itself in part originally determined by economic requirements. Following the conquest, European settlement occurred by preference in those areas where large settled populations of indigenous agriculturalists lived or where there were known deposits of precious metals. The ancestors of the present Negro populations of Latin America were brought to areas suitable for the growing of tropical products, especially sugar, for European markets. Although subsequent developments have modified the original pattern, the prime determinant of a country's social structure today is still the differing distribution from society to society of the socioracial groups that are the present-day successors of the biologically distinct racial groups of the sixteenth century, which themselves reflected the economic structure of the colonial period.

To approach problems of socioeconomic structure from the vantage point of the concept of "social race" enables one to achieve a much clearer understanding of some aspects of Latin American social reality. It is perfectly correct, for example, to point out that Latin American countries which differ in economic levels also tend to differ in certain other respects; for example, the countries with higher gross national products per capita tend, to some extent, to be more democratic. However, one can also ask: Why *do* countries have markedly different levels of gross national product per capita? One way of answering this question is to say that people of European ancestry generally live at one level of production and consumption, and Indians at another, much lower, level. Thus the predominantly European societies have higher gross national product levels than the Indian societies (with mulatto and mestizo societies in between the two), as Table 9 demonstrates.[3] This is bound to be so, given the substantial difference between European and Indian levels of living, even though the standard of living of the "white" in a predominantly Indian society may be higher than that of his cousin living in a predominantly European society. It is thus possible, in this example, to regard both economic levels and some of the sociopolitical characteristics of a society, such as its greater egalitarianism (which is one aspect of democracy), as both being in part dependent variables reflecting the underlying socioracial character of the society.

Clearly, the gross national product figures are only one index of the level of living generally prevalent in a country, and perhaps not always the best one, because of such factors as varying price levels and varying needs due to different climates and so on. If one takes life expectancy as a "composite" index of social welfare, however, as was done in the previous chapter, the differences in welfare levels among societies of different socioracial composition become even clearer, as Table 10 demonstrates. In this table, as in the one on gross national product, it is clear that different levels, in range, mean, and median, obtain in each group of societies. As in Table 9, there is no overlap between the ranges of the European and the Indian societies.

One of the interesting points that emerges from this kind of analysis is that the mulatto countries are clearly better off, even when data from Haiti are included, not only than the Indian countries but also than those characterizable as "mestizo." The writer would ascribe this to several factors, among them doubtless some fortuitous

TABLE 9

GNP Per Capita by "Racial" Character* of Society, 1957

Society	GROSS NATIONAL PRODUCT (U.S. DOLLARS)
European	
Argentina	$490
Uruguay	478
Costa Rica	357
mean: $441; median: $478	
Mulatto	
Venezuela	$648
Cuba	431
Panama	329
Brazil	293
Dominican Republic	239
Haiti	105
mean: $339; median: $311	
Mestizo	
Chile	$379
Colombia	263
El Salvador	219
Honduras	194
Nicaragua	160
Paraguay	114
mean: $221; median: $206	
Indian	
Mexico	$262
Ecuador	189
Guatemala	189
Peru	179
Bolivia	99
mean: $183; median: $189	

* Needless to say, statistics on "race" are of dubious accuracy and in any case are based on varying definitions from one country to another. For this reason the author has chosen to use categories rather than attempt to use quantitative statistics on race. Exact figures, are, however, given in the *Statistical Abstract for Latin America* published by the Center for Latin American Studies at UCLA and also, for most countries, by Yvan Labelle and Adriana Estrada, *Latin America in Maps, Charts, Tables,* CIF Study 1 (Cuernavaca: Center of Inter-Cultural Formation, 1963), p. 77. The author has hazarded his own nonnumerical estimates in *Latin American Politics in Perspective* (Princeton: Van Nostrand, 1963), pp. 21–22. Gross national product figures are those used by Bruce Russett *et al., World Handbook of Political and Social Indicators* (New Haven, Conn.: Yale University Press, 1964).

TABLE 10

Life Expectancy at Birth and Socioracial Composition

Society	LIFE EXPECTANCY
European	
Uruguay	66.5
Argentina	65.0
Costa Rica	59.0
mean: 63.5; median: 65.0	
Mulatto	
Cuba	59.0
Panama	56.5
Venezuela	55.0
Brazil	54.0
Dominican Republic	47.0
Haiti	42.5
mean: 52.3; median: 54.5	
Mestizo	
Chile	54.5
Paraguay	54.0
Nicaragua	52.5
Colombia	50.5
El Salvador	50.0
Honduras	47.5
mean: 51.5; median: 51.5	
Indian	
Mexico	53.5
Peru	51.5
Ecuador	45.5
Guatemala	43.0
Bolivia	40.5
mean: 46.8; median: 45.5	

SOURCE: Data on life expectancy are from the *Statistical Supplement* to ECLA's *Economic Bulletin for Latin America* for October 1962, via Bruce Russett, *et al.*, *World Handbook of Political and Social Indicators* (New Haven, Conn.: Yale University Press, 1964), pp. 197–198.

characteristics of the export markets for which some of the mulatto countries produce. But the mulatto societies appear to exhibit greater social and economic equality not only than the traditional Indian but also than the mestizo societies, perhaps because as (forced) immigrants, the

Negro populations were less rooted in their ancient ways of doing things, and perhaps because, with the abolition of slavery, even the sharecropper or tenant relation which the freed Negro assumed with relation to his former master gave him a social position superior to the effective serfdom which continued to exist in the predominantly Indian countries.[4]

Data on income inequalities are extremely hard to come by.[5] It is possible, however, to arrive at some estimate of inequality in income distribution by looking at the percentage of the national income which is paid in wages and salaries rather than going to profits, dividends, interest, and rent; that is, the share of a country's income going to labor rather than to capital. The higher the proportion paid in wages and salaries, the more equally the national income is distributed among the population. Although the data here are not complete and must be gleaned from several sources, nevertheless the substantial differences demonstrated by Table 11 constitute a strong indication of the radically different levels of equality prevailing between the different types of society, especially between the European and mulatto societies on the one hand and the mestizo and Indian societies on the other.

The life expectancy and income distribution figures given in Tables 10 and 11 suggest characteristics of social structure which tend to be overlooked by those who think in terms of gross national product or gross national product per capita figures alone. Thus, Chile and Colombia are usually regarded as relatively advanced countries in terms of economic standards, politics, and cultural life; it is useful to be reminded about the facts of social inequality which lie beneath the surface—as Germán Arciniegas put it, of the "invisible America" that lies beneath the "visible America." [6]

What are the implications for political analysis of the classification of the societies of Latin America into socio-racial types? In the first place, this approach serves as the necessary connecting link in the argument developed in the last chapter, in showing why higher levels of political

TABLE 11

Proportion of National Income Distributed as Wages
and Salaries, by Socioracial Composition

Society	PERCENTAGE
European	
Costa Rica	62%
Argentina	54
Uruguay	—
mean: 58.0%; median: 58.0%	
Mulatto	
Panama	68%
Cuba	64
Venezuela	61
Brazil	43
Dominican Republic	—
Haiti	—
mean: 59.0%; median: 62.5%	
Mestizo	
Honduras	44%
Chile	41
Paraguay	—
Nicaragua	—
Colombia	40
El Salvador	—
mean: 41.6%; median: 41.0%	
Indian	
Ecuador	49%
Peru	39
Mexico	—
Guatemala	24
Bolivia	—
mean: 37.3%; median: 39.0%	

SOURCE: Data are for 1950, except for Venezuela (1960). They are com-
puted from figures given in ECLA's *Boletín Estadístico de América
Latina*, Vol. II, No. 1 (March 1965), for Argentina, Brazil, Colombia,
Costa Rica, Ecuador, Guatemala, Honduras, and Panama; and in the
Statistical Supplement to the *Economic Bulletin for Latin America* of
November 1961, for Cuba and Peru; and of October 1959, for Chile.
Where data for later years were available, the percentages given appeared
to stay about the same or rise slightly, except for that of Argentina, which
seems to have been dropping steadily since the overthrow of Perón.

development are expressed in either greater constitutional stability or greater participation on terms of equality. The countries with an appreciable Indian component—those included in either Indian or mestizo categories above—especially when they have not experienced a thoroughgoing social revolution, are more inclined to hierarchy, social deference, and acceptance of government and less inclined to mass participation in politics than the more egalitarian European and mulatto countries. Economic development is correlated with political development; but Indian societies enjoy greater constitutional stability, relative to other Latin American societies, than one would expect on the basis of their economic development levels alone, while mulatto countries are more turbulent than figures on economic levels would suggest. The discrepancy is accounted for by taking the disturbing effects of mass participation on stability, in developing societies, into account; and the degree of participation reflects the (racially defined) degree of equality in the social structure. We turn now to a detailed consideration of distinctive political characteristics attributable to the socioracial character of the different countries, taking each category in turn.

The basic sociopolitical feature of the traditional, or unrevolutionized, Indian societies is the drastic subordination of a large segment of the population in a status separated by a considerable social distance from the dominant class, with the Indian on the whole passively accepting his position of subordination. The Indian's stolid acceptance of his weakness and suffering has long been noted by observers and has recently been confirmed by more systematic research by psychological anthropologists. William T. Mangin writes of the "relatively severe depression" noted not only in the Lima slum he surveyed but throughout Peru: "The humble, passive, tranquil, modest individual described by many informants as the ideal personality type is not strong and forebearing but rather frightened and ineffective." [7]

The way in which these attitudes are perpetuated by the dynamics of home life and are related to the authoritarian behavior of the father has been described very effectively by Everett Hagen in his *On the Theory of Social Change*.[8] Although the docility of the Indian is thus of course formed by early training and buttressed by cultural norms, it can also be regarded as a rational mode of adaptation to the realities of the social structure.[9]

This type of personality, normally stolid and passive in his relations with his social superiors, can also break out into sporadic anomic violence.[10] It should be noted, however, that when this violence occurs, it is a hopeless expression of protest foredoomed to ineffectualness, as Jorge Icaza has shown in his fictional treatment of an Indian uprising in Ecuador, *Huasipungo*. This ineffectual, anomic explosion of violence on the part of Indians pushed beyond their psychological limits is of course quite distinct from the calculated, organized, and purposive political violence that is a common feature of Latin American politics.

Given the usual docility of the Indian population, it is not surprising that the Indian societies in Latin America tend to exhibit greater constitutional stability than those of predominantly mestizo or mulatto character. Within the elite class of politically effective "whites," the rules of the constitutional game are reinforced by a sense of class solidarity, by interconnecting family ties, by upper class etiquette, and by commitment to family tradition and the need to uphold the family's good name. George Blanksten has referred to this observance of the constitutional rules within a narrowly circumscribed group as "Greek democracy." [11]

The brutal fury of the occasional revolts of desperate Indians, however, serve to remind the upper class Peruvian or Ecuadorean from time to time of the fragility of his political order and of the limited value of its guarantee of the safety of his life and property. The specter of Indian revolt is raised anew by threats to expand political participation, which raise the possibility of political changes in unknown directions that may possibly get out of hand and lead eventually to "stirring up" the Indians. The pattern of constitutional rule in which power is passed, often peacefully and legally, from one upper class clique to another is disturbed when a populist "traitor to his class" appears who attempts to build his political career on an appeal to the masses—not, of course, to the Indian masses, but to the mestizo masses in the cities. This threatened expansion of the effective polity raises the possibility of disorder, which may extend to the Indians, and in any case suggests the loss of control by the upper class, which presents unacceptable risks.

The role of the populist who tries to appeal to the urban masses has been played by Haya de la Torre in Peru, by Velasco Ibarra in Ecuador, and by Arévalo in Guatemala. When such a populist threat arises, it becomes necessary to break the constitutional rhythms of upper class democracy with military intervention designed to forestall the effective expansion of the polity. It should be noted that military intervention in this context is undertaken by the army as, in effect, agent of the upper class and not by a personalist or merely opportunistic clique of officers, which occurs more often in the mulatto countries.

Two of the Indian countries—Mexico and Bolivia—have, of course, experienced revolutions which began the process of integrating the Indians into national life. It should be noted, however, that even after political leaders committed to the integration of the Indians come to power, political stability can still be maintained. Despite the revolutionary legislation of the recent Mexican and Bolivian governments, one should not lose sight of the fact that the colossal social, economic, and cultural rigidities of the prerevolutionary era largely continue in existence, yielding only slowly to the government's efforts, however massive, to change them. Thus the revolution does not *in itself* change conditions as much as it does government orientation on policy questions, and popular attitudes and beliefs about social mobility.[12] Mexico's change in the latter respect is shown clearly by contrast with Colombia, as Andrew Whiteford points out in his comparative study of a Mexican and a Colombian town.[13]

What this means, politically speaking, is that in a postrevolutionary Indian society the population has begun to be socially mobilized and politicized but the social and economic conditions most conducive to democracy have not yet been fully brought into existence.

As Daniel Goldrich has pointed out,[14] there are different *modes* of political socialization; and while the new participants in politics are politicized as strong supporters of a revolutionary ideology of equality and progress, this can occur in either an institutionalist or a personalist mode. Loyalty may be given not to the institutions which the revolution creates to effect its purposes, but to individual revolutionary heroes. This has clearly been occurring in most of the "developing" countries.

Thus the elite dominance of the prerevolutionary Indian societies may be succeeded by the postrevolutionary personality cult of some leading figure. This tendency has been surmounted, after much turbulence, in Mexico through the institutionalization of the dominant revolutionary party under Plutarco Elías Calles, reinforced by Lázaro Cárdenas' subsequent rejection of Calles when Calles attempted to resume his political primacy. In Bolivia, similarly, Víctor Paz Estenssoro attempted to reimpose his personal authority on the revolution at the expense of its institutionalization when he had the constitution amended in 1964 to permit his successive reelection to the presidency. It did not appear to augur well for the institutionalization of the Bolivian revolution that Paz was thwarted by a combination of forces out of which emerged dominant not the reaffirmation of institutionalizing tendencies but instead the rival personalism of General René Barrientos Ortuño; but Barrientos subsequently stressed the necessity of institutionalization, specifically citing the need to follow the Mexican example.[15]

In many respects the mestizo countries show resemblances to those predominantly Indian; several of them in fact contain enclaves of unassimilated Indians, although the latter do not reach numbers sufficient to determine the character of the national social structure. Political participation in the mestizo countries is limited, as is suggested by the figures on electoral participation given in Table 12, but is not as restricted as in the "prerevolutionary" Indian countries. It should be noted that at the time of writing two of the mestizo countries, Chile and Colombia, continue to disenfranchise illiterates; only one of the mulatto countries, Brazil, and none of the European countries, does so. The prohibition on the voting of illiterates is, of course, characteristic of the prerevolutionary Indian countries; in Peru and Ecuador illiterates do not vote; in Guatemala, until 1965, male illiterates might vote but were not guaranteed a secret ballot—in other words, others could cast their votes for them.

It should be remembered that electoral participation is only one aspect of political participation, although the extent of the one is probably a good index of the extent of the other. One might expect the legal provisions relating to voting to be determining, reducing the social significance of the turnout figure and eliminating its value as an index of political participation in general, but apparently legal provisions do not have a controlling effect. Thus, for example, in Chile registration and voting are compulsory for those eligible, and the law provides for fines and imprisonment for violators. Nevertheless, under the same eligibility rules, the proportion of the population actually voting in the presidential elections doubled from 1952 to 1964; from 15.95 percent in 1952 to 31.82 percent in 1964.[16] The legal provisions were clearly not the controlling factors. The electoral participation figures of Table 12 are remarkable for the clarity with which they bear out the thesis that political participation is a function of degree of social equality, which in the Latin American societies is indicated by their socioracial structure. It should be noted that in the figures given in Table 12 there is virtually no overlap between the ranges of participation characteristic of European societies, of mestizo societies, and of traditional Indian societies, respectively, although the figures for the mulatto and postrevolutionary Indian countries complicate the picture.

If the prerevolutionary Indian countries seem at times to

TABLE 12
Electoral Participation,* by Socioracial Type

Society	PERCENTAGE VOTING	YEAR
European		
Argentina	44.8%	1958
Uruguay	36.4	1958
Costa Rica	28.6	1962
mean: 36.6%; median: 36.4%		
Mulatto		
Venezuela	43.1%	1958
Dominican Republic	32.2	1962
Haiti	28.3	1957
Cuba	25.0	1954
Panama	23.0	1960
Brazil	19.1 †	1960
mean: 28.5%; median: 30.2%		
Mestizo		
Nicaragua	30.6%	1963
Paraguay	25.8	1963
Honduras	19.2	1957
Chile	17.8 †	1958
El Salvador	16.0	1962
Colombia	15.5 †	1962
mean: 20.7%; median: 18.1%		
Postrevolutionary Indian		
Bolivia	28.0%	1960
Mexico	23.0	1958
Traditional Indian		
Ecuador	14.4 †	1960
Guatemala	13.9 ‡	1958
Peru	12.3 †	1958
(all Indian) mean: 18.3%; median: 14.4%		

* Percentage of population voting in relatively free presidential or general election close in time to 1960.

† Illiterates might not vote.

‡ Illiterate females might not vote; illiterate males might vote, but secrecy was not required for their ballots.

SOURCE: Yvan Labelle and Adriana Estrada, *Latin America in Maps, Charts, Tables,* CIF Study 1 (Cuernavaca: Center of Inter-Cultural Formation, 1963), p. 230, except for figures on Cuba, Nicaragua, Paraguay, and the Dominican Republic, which are calculated by the author from population figures given by Russett, *op. cit.,* pp. 18–20, and election results given in the *Hispanic American Report* for February 1963 (Dominican Republic) and April 1963 (Nicaragua and Paraguay). The figure for Cuba is from the *Statistical Abstract for Latin America, 1956* (Berkeley and Los Angeles: University of California Press, 1957).

be still in the sixteenth century, the mestizo countries give, in many respects, the impression of remaining in the eighteenth or nineteenth century. The partisan conflict in four out of the six mestizo countries remains basically that prevalent in the nineteenth century, a struggle between the traditional Conservative and Liberal parties. Of the fourteen other Latin American countries, only Uruguay continues the classic two-party system.[17] The mestizo countries where the party battle is basically that between Conservatives and Liberals are Columbia, Paraguay, Honduras, and Nicaragua. In these countries, strong party identification has the character of a polarization of opinion in preparation for combat rather than for the peaceful competition for the allegiance of the center of the political spectrum characteristic of two-party systems in developed countries. In the developed countries, the dynamics of two-party competition strengthens the moderate leadership in both parties. Where party rivalry reaches the extremes of combat or preparation for combat, on the other hand, extremist leadership is strengthened, as can be seen in the fanatic clericalism of the Colombian Conservatives under Laureano Gómez and the preference for authoritarian military rule of the Honduran or Paraguayan Conservatives.

The dominance of politics by the traditional parties suggests that social forces strong elsewhere are weak in the mestizo countries. This appears borne out by analysis of the case of organized labor. As was indicated by the figures given in Table 8 in Chapter Five, one may calculate that even in Chile, socially and economically the most advanced among the mestizo countries, the percentage of the population enrolled in unions around 1960 was only 6.5 percent, which placed Chile sixth in percentage unionized among the Latin American countries. In Colombia, 2.2 percent of the population was unionized, and in the other mestizo countries even less.

In Chile, where the two-party system has been submerged by twentieth-century events and forces, there have been no military seizures of power since the Depression. El Salvador, the other mestizo country without a basically two-party system, has known hardly any method of political change in recent years except seizure of power by one military group or another. It is significant that the occasions and forms of military intervention in the other mestizo countries are dominated and structured by the basic two-party split. That is, military intervention in politics or military rule occurs either in the name of one of the parties or in the name of putting an end to an excess of conflict between the two parties which has resulted in civil strife. Thus in Colombia the coup d'état staged by General Rojas Pinilla in 1953 was clearly intended to end the endemic fighting between Conservatives and Liberals that had mounted in intensity during the vindictively Conservative regime of Laureano Gómez. In Nicaragua, the personalist and then dynastic rule of the Somoza family operated through the medium of the Liberal party. In Honduras, the interests of the army are identified with those of the Nationalist party, through which military regimes rule; for their part, the Liberals make the elimination of the special position of the military, which amounts to freedom from civilian control, a leading Liberal principle. The Paraguayan picture is rather more complicated, but the military has ruled for some time through the traditional Colorado (Conservative) party.

In these countries the intermittent warfare between Conservatives and Liberals that characterized most of Latin America in the middle of the nineteenth century can still be found, and individuals are socialized into an intense party identification by recruitment for the party battle. What Charles W. Anderson has written of Nicaragua could be equally well said of Colombia or Honduras:

The civil wars of Nicaragua have not been the exclusive province of a small political elite, which left the rest of the nation relatively untouched. Insurrection in Nicaragua has not usually been an urban phenomenon. Revolts have more often been staged and fought in the hinterlands than in the streets and barracks of Managua. Thus, the country dweller has been brought into the political life of the nation, albeit with a rather unpropitious perspective.[18]

As Richard S. Weinert has shown in a recent article on *la violencia* in Colombia,[19] social change may intensify, instead of submerging, the bipartisan conflict as Conservative defense of the traditional order and its symbols becomes more desperate as the threats to it become greater.

In the mulatto countries, as the figures on the proportion of national income going to wages and salaries, on union membership, and on electoral participation suggest, there appears to be greater social equality and much less rigidity in the social structure than in the Indian or even in the mestizo countries. In the mulatto countries, class divisions are no more than that, not yawning gulfs between different linguistic, cultural, and racial groups. In both Brazil and Haiti, the subordination of "racial" criteria to those of class is suggested by the wry Brazilian folk saying to the effect that a poor white is a Negro and a rich Negro is a white or by its Haitian equivalent, which substitutes "mulatto" for "white."

One could not say the same thing in the Indian countries; "a rich Indian is a white" would be all wrong. There are no rich Indians; or, better, a white would not know a rich Indian from a poor one. His criteria of wealth are not the same as those of the Indian,[20] the communications gap between them is so great, and in any case an Indian becomes a "white" not by making money but by changing his language, residence, style of dress, and way of life.

The greater social mobility and the less entrenched character of the upper classes have various consequences in the mulatto societies, three of which we will note. In the first place, the *relative* absence of an entrenched traditional Hispanic upper class means also the *relative* absence of a governing class ethic with its sense of noblesse oblige. Thus there seems little doubt that it is countries in this socioracial category in which political graft reaches its most flagrant heights. Of course in this connection one has to do without published statistics; the impressionistic evidence seems strong, however. One remembers, among the recent Latin American dictators, Pérez Jiménez of Venezuela, Batista of Cuba, and Trujillo of the Dominican Republic and their multimillions; none of them was of upper class origin.

Brazil and Panama are notorious for more "democratic," more widely distributed graft taking. Thus one of the characteristics which made Jânio Quadros stand out from among Brazilian politicians was his honesty. One leading Brazilian figure, several times elected state governor, responded to a heckler's accusation that he stole public funds, "Yes, I steal, but I also build; the others steal, but they leave nothing to show for it." In Panama, it was reported in the early days of the Alliance for Progress that opposition members of the political class complained that the administration in power was being unfair because it proposed for Alliance approval the juiciest projects available, leaving relatively poor opportunities for graft to succeeding administrations. One recent Panamanian foreign minister appears to have handled relations with the United States in part so that his slaughter house interests would benefit from Canal Zone meat purchases, and a recent president, one of whose first official acts was to secure United States assistance for the Panamanian sugar industry, happened coincidentally to be the leading owner of sugar-producing land in the country.

With the exception of Brazil, the weakness of social restraints in the mulatto countries seems to result in greater brutality and violence in politics. Trujillo's massacres and tortures are matters of common knowledge, as is the brutality shown to rebel supporters during the Dominican civil war of 1965 by Trujillo's former generals. But even the more economically and socially developed Cuba had its own characteristic political gang warfare during the 1930s and 1940s. The Venezuelan far left has engaged in ruthless campaigns of terrorism since the overthrow of Pérez Jiménez, himself noted for the brutality of his regime. In the less dictator-ridden Panamanian environment, political violence takes the form of intermittent gunfighting among leading Panamanian politicians, including cabinet members and presidential candidates, especially during election periods.

The relative absence of the complex and time-encrusted class structure of Peru or Ecuador or the deep party loyalties of Colombia or Honduras means that military intervention in the mulatto countries takes predominantly opportunistic and personalist forms. In Peru or Colombia, an Odría or a Rojas Pinilla may intervene in politics in the name of a more or less united armed forces in response to a breakdown of constitutional processes; even a Somoza can rule in the name of an established political party and its historical tradition. But what did Trujillo or Pérez Jiménez or Batista represent except a lust for power and loot?

In the mulatto countries, especially in the Spanish-speaking ones, politics thus tends to be more turbulent, personalist, and violent than in the other Latin American countries; the prevalent patterns are for fluctuating multipartyism, opportunistic military intervention, and repressive personal dictatorship.

There is questionable value in generalizing about the political processes of the three Latin American countries whose populations are predominantly of unmixed European ancestry, since they are only three and the problems which face them are quite diverse. In Argentina, Uruguay, and Costa Rica, there is clearly no problem of the cultural integration of a subordinate Indian caste, nor of bringing the masses up to a level at which they will possess the basic skills requisite for participation in democratic politics. If the predominantly European countries do share a set of problems which lends common features to their political processes, it is that of maintaining the relatively high wages and social welfare benefits that obtain, since these are at the same time costs that tend to inhibit the rises in production necessary to continue to finance them. In Argentina and Uruguay, the problem has become that of economic stagnation, with increasingly illusory high wage levels and welfare benefit levels financed out of inflation, which in its turn reinforces the tendencies to stagnation. The problem is, of course, acutely political in Argentina, where it remains difficult to reintegrate a labor sector still loyal to Peronism into democratic politics, especially at a time when the relative value of the proportion of the national income going to labor has steadily deteriorated from the high point reached under Perón. In Uruguay, the economic problem is similar, although the political problem is far less acute. Uruguay, whose economy has a small resource and energy base, producing under conditions of labor indiscipline for a small overprotected market, cannot produce enough to support the very high level of welfare benefits and the large service, especially government service, sector of the economy.

In Costa Rica, the structure of the economic pressures is rather different: population growth in Costa Rica is at one of the highest rates in the world, while the population in Uruguay and Argentina grows hardly at all. The possibilities of providing for the country's growing population are limited under the conditions of the traditional coffee export economy, yet the possibilities of export diversification are severely limited because Costa Rica has much higher labor costs than its Central American neighbors, whose economies are booming, partly under the stimulus of regional market arrangements.

V
Mastering Change

Seven:
STRATEGIES OF
POLITICAL CHANGE

Although political development, understood in the sense used here, is strongly correlated with economic development, there is enough indeterminacy in the relationship that a variety of possible paths remain open for creative statesmanship. Accordingly, it makes sense, if one wishes to retain the insights which come from using the concept of political development while examining alternative political strategies, to think not in terms of a single track along which countries develop politically, but rather of areas of common origin and destination which they share; but a country may pass from one zone to the other by taking different routes.

The situation of a country undergoing political development might thus be compared to the situation of a man wanting to go from the New York area to the San Francisco area. The fastest and most direct way to go may be to fly nonstop; but he may prefer to go by train; or he may not be able to afford the fare and have to hitchhike. He may be delayed in Chicago by weather conditions, and he may misread his map and take a long detour. Thus at any one time a group of people who have left New York for San Francisco may be at different places and may appear to be moving in different directions; but in a longer perspective they are all headed westward, and the intention of each is to end up near San Francisco.

Similarly, states undergoing development have all started out from one form or another of "traditional society" which was stable and in which status was largely ascribed at birth; and the policies they find themselves following share the same premises: the attainment of a mass participation polity, the promotion of economic development, and the establishment of a welfare state.

In the case of the Latin American countries the facts of common origin and common destination are even clearer. The countries of the area began their independent existences with similar heritages from the colonial period; they continue to form part of a single cultural area and share a common set of values and aspirations.[1]

If the problem is stated in this general fashion, it is probably not necessary to make a special case of Cuba under Castro.[2] The writer does not doubt that the ultimate objectives of the Cuban leadership are freedom and justice as much as welfare and mass participation, just as the ultimate goals of Marx himself were not so different from those of the nineteenth-century liberals against whom he fought. The Cuban case can thus be regarded as an example of a very long detour on the route from New York to San Francisco, a detour in which the traveler seems to be going east rather than west for much of his journey; but an easterly halting place need not be regarded as journey's end. The Soviet Union itself has not finished its evolution, after all, and it may end up in a position not altogether different from that of the Western European and North American countries. It makes a great deal of sense, in fact, as Adam Ulam[3] and others have pointed out, to regard authoritarian socialism as one technique of transition from traditionalism to modernism and thus to regard the Stalinist state as pre-bourgeois rather than post-bourgeois.

There are four general types of ways in which structural social and political change can be brought about; which, if any, will be followed depends on the constraints imposed by the external situation, but also partly on choices made by the important political actors. The four avenues to change are as follows:

1. *Revolutionary and postrevolutionary innovation from above* consists of the direct and deliberate introduction of changes by an innovating elite after the balance of forces has been shifted, usually by violence, to eliminate or greatly reduce the possibilities of opposition and obstruction. Social revolution thus takes place in two phases: first, the drastic reordering of power relations among social groups; second, the introduction of structural changes that this shift in power relations makes possible.

2. *Evolutionary innovation from above* does not necessarily differ from revolutionary innovation in the goals sought, or in the fact that changes are introduced by an elite, but rather in that the innovators operate within the preexisting structure of legal and constitutional rules. That is, evolutionary innovation takes place with a minimum, or even a total absence, of violence, and existing procedural norms are on the whole respected; for example, those guaranteeing individual liberties and the right of compensation for expropriated property. Because it accepts these constraints on action, evolutionary innovation is necessarily slower, more difficult to achieve, and, perhaps, less effective than revolutionary innovation. Nevertheless the latter also suffers from several typical weaknesses which will be considered subsequently.

3. *Innovation through concessions to pressure from below* may take place in some cases only in response to acts of violence, depending on the degree of commitment of the ruling group to the status quo.

4. *Innovation by compromise and bargaining between groups neither one of which is subordinate to the other* can take place in some types of postrevolutionary situations or in the founding of a new state by emigrants, where

conflict is not between entrenched and innovating elements but between coordinate segments of the group constructing new institutions.

Let us now consider each category of deliberate political change in detail.

Revolutionary Innovation

The prospect of conducting a revolution from above, that is, of being able to introduce structural changes without having to operate under procedural constraints, exerts a powerful attraction on those dedicated to reform. It is patently much simpler to be able to innovate without having to secure legislative majorities, without having to face lengthy challenges in the courts, and without having to respect the property rights of vested interests. Because of these factors, it is always possible that a government originally committed to evolutionary innovation will turn to revolutionary procedures when it finds out how great the obstacles to innovation are—provided it has a monopoly of effective force and thus has only its own preferences to guide its choice of how to proceed. This type of factor seems to account for the change in orientation undergone by the regime of Fidel Castro in Cuba during its first two years in power. It requires considerable self-restraint on the part of an innovating leadership that monopolizes power to allow its programs to be resisted and delayed solely for the sake of procedural norms, when these are accorded a lower degree of preference than the leadership's goals of structural reform.

The irony of revolutionary innovation, already amply displayed in the classic cases of the French and Russian revolutions and now becoming clearly apparent in the Cuban case, is that a monopoly of force and a clear perception of ultimate goals are not in themselves adequate to transform those goals into reality, for three principal reasons.

In the first place, if the regime relies upon its monopoly of force to achieve revolutionary objectives, the maintenance of that monopoly becomes essential for the functioning of the regime. Yet the attempt to maintain total control has a dynamic of its own; it posits objectives of its own contradictory to, and eventually substituting for, the goals of the revolution themselves. The paradoxical outcomes of attempts at revolutionary innovation are only too well known. A revolution to free the individual from the fetters of unreasonable medieval restraints leads to Fouché and Napoleon; a revolution to free men from exploitation and to usher in an era of perfect freedom leads to the NKVD and Stalin.

In the second place, the opposition which revolutionary regimes seek to eliminate has functions over and above that of simple obstruction. A regime that lacks an opposition lacks also the necessity to consider carefully what it is doing, lacks the necessity for justifying its actions, and lacks early warning of its mistakes. The colossal tactical and policy errors of Stalin (and, for that matter, of Khrushchev) are now becoming better and better known and have indeed been acknowledged by the Soviet regime—after those who perpetrated them have left the scene. In the revolutionary government of Cuba, Major Guevara acquired a certain reputation for plain speaking by frequently devoting his speeches to criticisms of mistakes made by himself and his colleagues in the past.[4]

In the third place, the existence of total control typically has counterproductive results in the economic sphere, since the lack of a free market system renders the rational allocation of resources difficult and the elimination or attenuation of the profit motive reduces incentives to higher productivity. The Soviet economic system has long sought to create a functional equivalent for profits in the shape of premium payments for fulfillment of planned norms; while the more recent innovations associated with the name of Professor Liberman and tending in a free-market direction indicate that the economic value of economic freedom is appreciated by the Soviet leadership.

The whole ethos of a revolutionary leadership is precisely to reject the past, however, and to assume that the regularities prevailing before the revolution were characteristic only of the preexisting system and not of economic necessity in general. This extreme relativism is given support by the evidence of the public-spirited and even puritanical behavior of the revolutionaries themselves, and of young people generally, in the days following the revolution. After the revolution is victorious, however, revolutionary fervor becomes less relevant to the daily tasks of administration and production, and behavior, unable to maintain the pitch and moment of those first days, tends to show again the characteristics of self-serving expediency of the period before the revolution.

Nevertheless, revolutions typically insist on making their own mistakes and refusing to learn from the experience of others. After making their own mistakes, however, and coming to appreciate that the laws governing social phenomena cannot be abolished by revolutionary decrees, the revolution can move in one of two directions. It can give up its original social goals in practice (although lip service to them is of course always given) and become on the whole simply a system for the maintenance of totalitarian power; or it can allow the total monopoly of power to erode in the interest of the implementation of the revolution's social goals. If the latter option is taken, however, greater freedom is allowed, the regime gradually places itself under procedural restraints, and the system comes progressively to approximate what it would have been had the leadership chosen the evolutionary road in the first place. For this reason, the writer feels justified in considering the revolutionary path chosen by Cuba, for example, as one that may yet lead toward the same ultimate destination as that of countries undergoing political development along different paths.

Evolutionary Innovation

Evolutionary innovation attempts to work within the existing constitutional and legal framework. Compared with revolutionary innovation, therefore, its programs of reform suffer from four principal disadvantages.

1. Reforms involving changes in property relations are more expensive because of the need to compensate former property owners.

2. It is more difficult to secure the passage of enabling legislation, because an effective legislature exists with guarantees for the freedom of opposition activities.

3. Delay and even total obstruction in the implementation of new programs is made possible by means of continuous appeals to an autonomous judiciary. This drawback is generally intensified by an antireform bias in the judiciary due both to the personal political orientations of its personnel and to the conservative nature of its institutional role.

4. The maintenance of the reforming administration in power is problematical. The conservative opposition is more likely to be entrenched in crucial positions in the communications media—the newspapers, radio broadcasting, and religious pulpits—from which it can exert influence to provoke popular opposition to the regime and thus contribute to its electoral defeat. The conservative opposition is also likely to have access to the top echelons of the military institution and will attempt to use its influence in that quarter to provoke a military coup d'état against the regime. The elements of common interest between right-wing civilian politicians and members of the military leadership stratum are several. High-ranking military officers tend to identify with upper-status civilian elements, regardless of their own social origins;[5] a military force used primarily for domestic policing has an institutional bias toward the maintenance of order and the preservation of the *status quo*; while a democratic reformist program necessarily envisages the strengthening of civilian control of the military, which may threaten the place of the military institution in the existing social order, as well as the personal prerogatives of high-ranking officers.[6]

The greatest obstacle in the path of a government of an evolutionary innovative tendency is of course the possibility of being removed from office, by either constitutional or extraconstitutional means.

An extraconstitutional removal from office can be especially damaging, not only in itself, but also because movements of the center-left are comparatively ill-adapted to the violent political combat, overt or covert, that then results. Protracted conflict has the inevitable outcome of polarizing opinion toward the extremes and undermining the position of the center. This has been demonstrated perfectly clearly in civil wars from Spain to the United States to China. It occurs also in situations of more covert conflict, as was shown, for example, by the considerable strengthening of the position of the French Communist party which occurred as a result of its performance in the resistance movement during the German occupation.

The prospects are quite different where political conflict remains within the ambit of constitutional procedures; political forces are then more likely to be equilibrated so that the center of gravity lies in the center-left of the political spectrum. It is of course well known that in situations where coalition governments are necessary, just as in committee deliberations, the occupants of a center position play a key role. This is attested by the legendary success of the Radical parties of France and Chile or by the remarkable career of René Pléven during the Fourth Republic.

In Latin America, accordingly, the ability of parties of center-left orientation to come to power and subsequently to remain in power seems dependent on whether or not they are able to occupy the political center of gravity rather than being located more toward the extreme of the spectrum of effective political opinion. Thus in the cases of the overthrow of Juan Bosch in the Dominican Republic or of the persistent refusal of the Peruvian military to allow the APRA to come to power, movements which would be regarded as center-left in orientation elsewhere were perceived by military leaders and conservative civilian politicians as left-wing, crypto-communist, and so on, and were prevented either from coming to power or from remaining in power. Forces that would be regarded as of the extreme left elsewhere were in these cases of negligible significance.

This type of situation contrasts strongly with the situation in Chile and Venezuela in recent years. When

Rómulo Betancourt took office in Venezuela in 1958 the odds were overwhelming that he would not be allowed to finish out his five-year term; no popularly elected civilian president had ever done so in Venezuela. What enabled Betancourt to survive was the existence of a militant and violent movement of the extreme left. By cracking down heavily on left-wing terrorism and taking a strong diplomatic position against the Castro regime in Cuba, Betancourt was able to differentiate his position clearly from that of the communists and procommunists. At the same time he was able to point out to the military leadership that the strategy of the far left was patently to try to provoke a military seizure of power so that political opinion would become polarized and the far left would be strengthened by participating in an underground resistance movement.[7] Faced with this configuration of circumstances, the military allowed Betancourt to finish out his term.

The dynamics of the Chilean situation were quite similar, despite the superficial lack of comparability between the two cases. Eduardo Frei led a Christian Democratic party of strongly reformist complexion, a party that in many situations would be kept out of power by a military-oligarchic alliance—even in Chile. In the Chilean election of 1964, however, the candidate of the Communist-Socialist alliance was generally thought to have an excellent chance of winning the election, and so Frei appeared to the voters on the right as the lesser of the two evils; thus much of the center and right rallied to Frei and his near-revolutionary program, ensuring his victory.

The ability of a party of center-left orientation to reach and hold power thus depends on the presence of a configuration of political circumstances which locates the party at the pivotal point of the political balance, as well as on the presence of tactical skills in the leadership which enable it to make use of this situation.

Concession to Pressure from Below

Structural change tending toward the attainment of a new equilibrium may also come about as a result of concessions made by the ruling group in response to pressure from below. The classic model of this type of change is provided by the extension of the suffrage during the nineteenth and early twentieth centuries in the countries of Western Europe. In Britain and Belgium, for example, each extension of the suffrage was preceded by riots and demonstrations which may have been regarded in some conservative circles as presaging violent revolution, as in the case of the Hyde Park riots, but made the consequences of a limited extension of the suffrage seem the lesser evil even if the alternative were only more violence and disorder.

To think in terms of the amount of violence either used or threatened as the sole determinant of outcomes of situations characterized by pressure from below would be to miss several other crucial variables, however. A calculation of the force available to each side does not in itself indicate outcomes because of a lack of symmetry between the two sides to the struggle in the valuation of the costs and benefits of the alternative possible outcomes. This type of factor has been very nicely isolated by the developers of game theory.

This lack of symmetry in the preference schedules of the two contending forces is due to three interrelated factors. First, the object in contention may be of greater value to the less privileged group. For example, the vote may be sought by the disenfranchised not primarily as a means of changing public policy but rather as a mark of heightened status. The extension of the suffrage to women would be a case predominantly of this character. The advantages of maintaining the status quo on this point could then seem relatively small to the ruling group, which would be likely to yield the point before the disadvantaged group had reached the upper limits of the unpleasantness it was prepared to create.

The outcome of clashes between pressure from below and resistance from above thus depends both on the amounts of force that each contender can bring to bear and on the readiness of each to use the maximum force available to him. The latter depends in turn on the contenders' conception of proper means and on their degree of commitment, in terms of both self-interest and ideology, to the objective over which they are fighting.

By its nature, change brought about as a result of concession to pressure is spread over a considerable period of time, conflict being joined and broken off intermittently. It should be noted that the combat does not necessarily take place on equal terms, as several dynamic tendencies favorable to political development and intrinsic to this kind of situation may become active. These tendencies arise out of the tension between norm and actuality, the competition for power among elite groups, and the inherent implausibility of certain institutional formulas.

The first of these tendencies favorable to political development arises from the tension between norm and actuality. There is a propensity for a political system to create an ideology that legitimizes the obedience of subjects to its authority. The doctrines of legitimacy which are generated may not be wholly supportive of constituted authority, however, for two reasons. The first, and less important, reason is that any system of doctrine, by virtue of being a system, implies regularity, orderly processes, and the equal treatment of persons defined as belonging to a single class or category. The institutionalization of a system of rule, even of class rule, thus inevitably implies the reduction or elimination of arbitrariness. Because an element of arbitrary rule does always exist, however, a certain tension, with a potentially destabilizing effect, is always present.

A second source of potential tension, of greater significance, lies in the fact that a doctrine of legitimacy is not generated autonomously by a political system solely to reflect its own requirements but that a tendency characteristically exists to incorporate elements of belief systems identified with countries of higher prestige. Thus at any one historical moment there are likely to be a limited number of idealized doctrines of legitimacy, each identified with a leading world power or group of powers. This in turn reflects the general tendency in international politics for any conflict between states (or, in other periods of time, other political entities) to be ideologized as a conflict of doctrines. From the wars recounted in the Bible, in which petty Middle Eastern monarchies and patriarchies fought each other in the name of their respective gods, to the conflicts between Greek and Persian, and Greek and Greek, down to the disputes of the twentieth century, men have tended to think of interstate conflict in ideological terms, even when yesterday's ally has become today's bitter enemy. It is therefore common for the avowed ideology of some major contender on the world scene to influence the formal belief systems of other states which identify with its cause or lie within its sphere of influence. These elements of borrowed ideology will then exert a destabilizing effect on actual political institutions. Since the more prestigious countries are likely to be the more advanced in terms of the economic, social, and political technology available, it is likely that the ideological principles borrowed from them exert their pull in the direction of a higher order of social and political development.[8]

A second inherent tendency toward political development arises where there is competition for power among different segments of a limited participant group. In this kind of situation, one of the contenders for power may seek to extend the arena by admitting new groups to participation: to escalate the political combat in the expectation that his forces will be augmented from the ranks of the new recruits. This tendency has been pointed out by various writers; nineteenth-century extension of the suffrage deriving from considerations of tactical advantage can plausibly be associated with the names of Jackson, Disraeli, and Bismarck.

At the same time, appreciation by those of higher status of the tendency for competition within a limited group of participants to lead to an expansion of the participant group may result not in an expansion of the arena but instead in an agreement not to compete. This is what occurred in the case of the Colombian National Front agreement that went into effect in 1958. Competition between

the Conservative and Liberal parties had become so acute
that fighting between partisans of the two was general in
many areas of the country. In order to avoid mass involvement of this kind and in order to foreclose the possibility
of military intervention, to which continued disorder constituted a standing invitation, the leaders of the two parties concluded a pact providing for the equal division of
inferior political offices and the alternation of the presidency between them.

A third intrinsic tendency toward political development
in a pressure/concession situation arises out of the tendency for certain compromise formulas to decay. Certain
sets of arrangements have a greater inherent plausibility
than others.[9] Once changes are made in some set of arrangements based on a clear and self-consistent principle,
change tends to continue until institutions come to reflect
some alternative principle. This occurs by means of a natural process of the elimination of anomalies and inconsistencies through the rationalizing effect of administrative
actions, through the application of rules developed in one
context to another by judicial decision, through the rationalizing effects of dialogue between or among the
political parties, and also through the tendency of individuals to eliminate inconsistencies among the various patterns of behavior they follow. The steady dilution of property requirements for voting in Western Europe during
the nineteenth century illustrates this general principle; so
does the failure to persist of systems of weighted voting
in the British African territories in more recent times.

This tendency for concession to lead to further concession is of course well known to extreme conservatives, who
thus dig in their heels against reform and refuse to budge.
By doing so, however, they run the risk of losing everything if the forces making for change prove to be too
strong. This is illustrated by the difference in the present
status of the Prussian Junkers, who refused to make concessions, and the British aristocrats, who knew how to
yield gracefully.[10]

The problem of the decay of implausible formulas exists also in international relations. In limiting a war, for example, the overwhelmingly plausible line of limitation in arena is a national boundary; in weapons, the distinction between the "conventional" and the "unconventional." Sophisticated strategic theorists can well argue that limitations of these kinds are arbitrary, and that therefore some other equally arbitrary criterion of limitation that provides a greater advantage for the contender of whom the strategist is a partisan should instead be used. The point is, however, that the plausibility of any given line of demarcation depends largely on nonrational connotations which it has; to ignore these because they are irrational opens up the possibility of unlimited escalation of the conflict.

Innovation by Compromise Among Reforming Groups

The three types of innovation previously discussed each assumes a set of people already lodged in leadership positions, whose actions then grow out of the interplay between intention and situation.[11] However, circumstances can obtain in which a government does not preexist but has to be created by a bargaining process among opposing forces none of which is committed to the status quo. Situations of this type occur, for example, when a state is newly founded by migrants from another country, when a successful revolution is made by a combination of disparate forces, when a country regains its autonomy after having been occupied by an enemy power, and so on. It may occasionally happen that in a case of this type the constituent group appoints a distinguished figure as legislator, a Solon or a Bolívar, and enacts his proposal without change. The much more common situation, however, is for agreement to derive from a process of give and take among elements representing different interests and points of view.[12]

A very great range of possible institutional arrangements exists, of course. From the point of view of political development, however, the set of institutions most likely to endure is one that both allows for the protection of vested interests and at the same time makes possible innovation to meet the changing demands of the external situation. Constituent bodies generally perceive the problem of constitution making in this light—to combine the power of effective action and the capacity to innovate, on the one hand, with the defense of established interests and legitimate minority rights, on the other. Clearly, it will not conduce to the ability of the system to last if either of these functions dominates the resulting instrument at the expense of the other. A set of arrangements which maximizes only the capacity to innovate and act effectively will resemble the system of revolutionary innovation described above and will fall prone to its characteristic defects, its tendency to arbitrariness and massive error. On the other hand, a system allowing for maximum defense of established rights makes innovation impossible, becomes immobilistic, and collapses when it fails to meet external or internal challenges. One has only to look at the history of France to find abundant evidence for each of these propositions, the colossal disasters of revolutionary and Bonapartist effort contrasting with the paralysis of the parliamentary republics, as France swings from one constitutional pole to the other.

The problem that confronts the constituent group is thus that of striking a balance between energy and inertia, between innovation and status quo, between powers and rights. It may of course happen that a constituent group is dominated by sophisticated political theorists who perceive the problem in these terms and, imbued with public spirit, disinterestedly create a balanced structure. It is much more likely, however, that the different elements participating represent groups with specific interests which lie either in maintaining the economic and social status quo or in seeking to revise it and who are therefore concerned to bias the resulting system in one or the other direction. If the representation of the two points of view is finely equilibrated a balanced set of institutions may result. A similar outcome is possible in the theoretically more interesting situation of equilibrium, not between the conservative and radical forces only, but between any two political parties or alliances. If it is not clear to each contender which of two leading political parties is likely to win control under the system that is being set up, then each is torn between conflicting desires. Each party wishes to assure itself of effective powers should it win control of the executive, but at the same time each wants to limit those powers should they be wielded by the opposition. It is thus possible for two parties which oppose each other on substantive grounds to be so evenly matched in a constituent body that they agree completely on the constitutional mechanisms to be adopted. This was almost the situation in the Parliamentary Council that drafted the Basic Law of the West German Federal Republic, in which the Christian Democrats and the Social Democrats each had the same number of representatives. The situation of a political party participating in the writing of a constitution without knowing if it will be in the majority or minority as a result of future elections resembles that of a gambler seeking to make a set of wagers which will together be likely to maximize his winnings and minimize his losses. The correct solution is thus what game theorists have called a "minimax" strategy. The rational strategy for constitution makers operating under conditions of uncertainty as to the identity of future occupants of positions of power (which is frequently the same as to say planning for a long period to come) is thus to choose a set of arrangements which combine the maximum capacity to meet new situations with the maximum protection for established interests. This is simply to reformulate the classic principle of normative political thought that the ideally best constitution provides for a mixed polity.[13]

If one turns from the theoretical analysis of the deliberate promotion of structural change to an examination of the concrete problems which such an enterprise has in the Latin American context, then it becomes apparent that the appropriateness of different possible strategies for an innovating group is determined by the sociopolitical structure; that is, by the character of the relations of dominance among social classes and forces, by the social balance of power. Looking at the modes by which institutional change can be achieved that were described above in this light, one would estimate the relative probabilities that one mode rather than another will be chosen along the following lines.

The fourth mode of achieving change discussed above, that is, as the outcome of compromise among groups coordinate in power in a "new" and unstructured political situation, can of course occur only under certain very special circumstances. The condition of coordinate power between constituent groups, neither of which is committed to the preexisting system, is most likely to be satisfied, in Latin America, in a two-party system following the departure from office of a dictator. It is thus most likely to occur in the two-party mestizo countries still susceptible to dictatorship—Honduras, Nicaragua, and Paraguay—just as it was in a country of this type, Colombia, that this mode of institutional reform was attempted, following the overthrow of General Rojas Pinilla in 1957. These countries are similar to Colombia in that the tendency of party conflict to degenerate into violence and guerrilla warfare has provided the occasion and justification for the imposition of personal dictatorship in the absence of interparty agreement on the rules governing party rivalry.

The great danger facing interparty agreements in systems of this type, as the Colombian example shows, is that they will become immobilist in policy terms. The new institutions created make partisan stalemate likely. Excessive concessions need to be made to conservatives who are fearful of change, less favorable to democratic institutions, and less averse to violence, in order to secure their adherence to the new system. And the leadership elements in the two parties concluding the new agreement conceive of the danger it is designed to preclude as that not simply of violence, but specifically of violence tending to disrupt or destroy the social and economic status quo in which they hold elite rank.

Fruitful use of the third mode of institutional change described above, that of the piecemeal securing of concessions which cumulatively represent a fundamental change, from a ruling group whose control of power is not directly and immediately threatened, by the maintenance of pressure "from below," does not seem likely. Conservative governments representing the possessing classes in Latin America typically do not make fundamental changes in response to pressure from below but rather interpret such pressure as portending the dangers of "social dissolution"—in the phrase used by the Mexican antisubversive law; while they may make concessions on minor economic or social welfare points, they are more likely to meet pressure for reforms which imply fundamental structural change with police measures. If weak governments, or governments sympathetic to the demands being posed— land reform, the enfranchisement of illiterates, or the definitive establishment of civilian control over the military, for example—appear to be ready to make concessions, then those governments are overthrown by military coups d'état, as Chapter Four has suggested.

The second possible mode of achieving change discussed above, evolutionary innovation, can occur in any type of country in which the sociopolitical balance permits relative freedom of maneuver to a moderate innovating group located at the left-center of the political spectrum. As pointed out above, these are the circumstances which appear to obtain currently in Chile and Venezuela. Needless to say, this path of action demands a high order of political skill on the part of evolutionary leaders maneuvering between the potential "gorillas" and the potential guerrillas. Circumstances which most favor effective action by such a group occur where opinion is not thoroughly polarized by extreme social and economic cleavage —that is, in the European and mulatto countries where, as a rule, greater equality of social conditions obtains.

The first mode of change discussed, revolutionary innovation, is most likely to occur when the extreme polarization of opinion has resulted in a divorce of the innovating group from the legal and political assumptions which previously characterized the social order. The revolutionary group perceives this structure of procedures and obligations as creating obstacles too great to allow basic change to proceed without revolution. This secession of the group desiring innovation from the social consensus is likely to occur in Latin America under three sets of circumstances: (1) where the social gulf between the possessing class and the lower classes appears too great to be modified by evolutionary means, that is, typically in the Indian countries; (2) where very substantial foreign interests are expected to obstruct change and to be backed by the power of their home government; and (3) where the dynamics of the political situation have led to combat, polarizing opinion, and destroying the middle ground in the political spectrum and along with it the possibility of consensus between left and right. This elimination of the middle position, which drives innovating groups to the revolutionary pole, can result from the experience of combat, or from repeated experience of the prevention of the implementation of a progressive program within a constitutional framework by military intervention or the rigging of elections. The pattern of rigged elections and military intervention was, for example, imposed on Argentina with the removal of the Radicals from office in 1930; thus the Peronist position, that social reform could not come about by constitutional and peaceful means, was rendered plausible. Similarly, the revolutionary position would have acquired substantial force in Venezuela if the military had not allowed Betancourt to operate from a middle position. It is thus most often the case that right-wing forces themselves bring about the schism in the political spectrum which strengthens the attraction of the revolutionary pole by taking the first steps in the destruction of constitutional processes and thus of the middle ground of evolutionary innovation.

A weaker form of this latter situation in which the middle position is not destroyed completely but is instead discredited for key segments of the reform movement is created when a period of constitutional politics under moderate leadership has been marked by graft, factionalism, and lack of achievement. Under these circumstances a tendency to extremism is created, even though revolution is not, strictly speaking, the only feasible reform strategy. This seems to have been the nature of the impact the period 1944–1952 in Cuban politics had on the thinking of Fidel Castro, whose active interest in politics began and developed during that period.

Needless to say, the United States often plays a major role in determining the direction which the political situation will take by using its influence in favor of one or the other of the alternatives it has by turns historically supported, the position of the evolutionary innovators or that of the irreconcilable anticonstitutional conservatives and military officers. In this connection, it should be noted that there is substantial irony in the argument given by some commentators in the attempt to reconcile these two alternative policies, that Latin American military officers may absorb democratic and constitutional ideas by being exposed to American influences. Exposure to American influences in this context means association with American military officers who have often turned out to be as narrow-minded, imperceptive, and authoritarian as their Latin American counterparts. Or it may be that the association between the two results in American military attachés' absorbing the values of their Latin American colleagues, rather than the reverse. For whatever reason, the political consciousness of the American military who are in contact with Latin American officers often extends no further than a naïve "anticommunism" which does not alter the penchant to military intervention and the destruction of the evolutionary position.

On the other hand, it should be noted that the well-known antipathy of the United States to revolutionary modes of innovation may serve to inhibit the revolutionary inclinations of innovating elites once in power and incline them more in the evolutionary direction. This seems to have been true in the Bolivian case, at least, and also to some extent in the Mexican.

It may at first glance seem paradoxical that one can talk about different strategies of bringing about political development and at the same time about autonomous secular economic and social forces with developmental results. What is the point of expending human effort in bringing about something that may be going to occur in any case? Marx answered this question using the "midwife" analogy: one could not alter the outcome, but one could assist at the birth and lessen the pains involved. Applied to historical forces, however, Marx's midwife imagery is inexact. A historical phenomenon is not like a baby, predetermined in its major characteristics. The appropriate analogy in the case of political development is surely that the role of the human participant resembles not that of the midwife but that of the manager of a river system. The waters of the rivers will seek their own level, they will flow downhill, and they will end up in the ocean; but the manner in which they arrive there can be changed by human acts— canals can be cut, river channels dredged, and dams built. Man's purposes relate to shorter-term outcomes than history's "purposes," after all. If man has the technology, then he also has the obligation, to divert the rivers of history this way or that in the interests of human values: to generate power, to irrigate land, to avoid destructive floods.

Eight:
TOWARD A
NEW EQUILIBRIUM

"Political development" was defined, for purposes of this study, as having the formal character of the attainment of stable constitutional functioning and, in our era, the substantive character of the expansion of participation on terms of equality. Although this is an adequate specification for operational purposes, it does not constitute an exhaustive description of the phenomenon, since several other important characteristics of a developed polity, while not logically entailed in the terms of the definition given, are nevertheless empirically associated with one or another of its components.

Thus mass participation in elections whose outcome is respected appears to require the maintenance of a system of assured civil liberties, since these are functionally related to the individual's autonomy as a participant and the candidates' ability to compete. The point was suggested by Justice Stone in the famous "footnote 4" to his opinion in *United States v. Carolene Products* and has been persuasively argued by C. W. Cassinelli.[1]

Another characteristic feature of a "developed" state today is the tendency for government policy to aim at the maximization of social welfare. This tendency clearly grows out of the dynamics of party competition under conditions of universal electoral participation.[2] If individuals tend to be valued equally as participants in politics, they tend to be valued equally as beneficiaries of policy. As Cassinelli puts it: "Welfare policy and civil liberties, which occur in all democratic states, are necessary parts of the democratic political complex, and they are directly related to one another as companion results of the dynamics of representative government." [3]

Accordingly, political development today may be described in terms not only of expanding participation but also of increasing actualization of the values of freedom and welfare.

If this is so, then there is clearly a point at which participation reaches an effective maximum, the posited values are actualized to the maximum permitted by the refractory nature of the human and social material, and a polity can be said to be in a developed state. In the terms used earlier in the book, the polity then reattains a condition of stable functioning; new equilibrium conditions have been reached. In the present era, this equilibrium situation is that of the "modern democratic state." In gross terms the system can then be described as stable, although this stability is not absolute, as will be noted below. Under the conditions prevailing in the current era, the "modern democratic state" is likely to remain on the whole stable for the following reasons:

1. A state of this character conforms most closely to the ideological modes now dominant in most of the world. Thus it is not subject to the destabilizing tension that exists where a set of political institutions embodies premises different from those of the prevailing ideological currents.

2. Even where democratic ideology is not positively espoused, however, the modern democratic state may nevertheless seem preferable to any alternatives. Under the circumstances of demythologization and secularization pre-

vailing today, the postulate of human equality underlying the institutions of the modern democratic state, even if perceived as arbitrary, seems nevertheless less arbitrary than the premises embodied in rival systems. This feeling, as well as an assessment of the relative quality of the modern democratic state's performance of its functions, is surely found in those lack-illusion *mots* of sophisticated democrats, like Churchill's "Democracy is the worst form of government, except for all the others," or James Fenimore Cooper's "We do not adopt the popular polity because it is perfect but because it is less imperfect than any other."

3. The modern democratic state's chances of survival seem further strengthened by the minimal nature of the consensus it requires to function, which apparently relates exclusively to procedural questions. It should be noted that even the "substantive" faith of the supporter of constitutional democracy is preeminently faith in procedures, elections, rules governing the exercise of political power, and rules governing the conduct of judicial proceedings.[4] This is clearly the conclusion of twentieth-century analysis of the character of the democratic state from A. D. Lindsay to such recent writers as Mayo, Dahl and Lindblom, Cassinelli, and Thorsen.[5] This essentially procedural-consensus nature of the modern democratic state makes it particularly well adapted to survival today, when the breakdown of authoritarian religious value systems under the impact of secularization and the breakdown of organic societies dominated by a single traditional cultural complex under the influence of the spread of world culture have led to a widespread privatization of values most compatible with a minimum-consensus state.[6]

4. One of the major factors making for stability in the modern democratic state is the fact that in it political participation is at an effective maximum, given the existence of universal adult suffrage. This means that it is not possible to destabilize the system by enfranchising new groups and thus radically shifting the balance of political forces. In a limited-participation state, on the other hand, the destabilizing effects of the expansion of participation are

always an active possibility because of the relative advantage in the political conflict that participation expansion would confer on one or another political party or on one or another embattled organ of government.

5. At the same time, the nature of the institutional structure of the modern democratic state is likely to render it more stable on the whole than other political forms. The institutional mix characteristic of the modern democratic state, with its balancing of mass participation, representation of interests, and guaranteed rights, approaches what was called in the previous chapter a "minimax" solution to the problem of combining the power necessary to take effective action with the restraints on power necessary to avoid the making of monumental blunders.

It was written above that the fully developed modern democratic state is *relatively* stable. Destabilization may, however, still occur, deriving from two different factors. In terms of the model of the stable political system developed in Chapter One, these can be identified as dissatisfaction with the policy output of the system and change in the structure of the set of participant groups.

The possibility of dissatisfaction with government policy derives from the fact that, because of the egalitarian welfare policies which mass political participation impels governments to follow, developed polities tend to become, if they are not already, mass consumption societies. If consumption takes place at the expense of future production, however, by diverting funds away from capital investment, it may eventually become necessary to restrict consumption in the interest of growth. This is the stage reached by Uruguay, regarded by general consent as the most politically developed state in Latin America. In Uruguay, a vast social welfare system, short working hours, early retirement, and government-subsidized consumption have accompanied peaceful successions to power (except for an interlude during the Depression), and an extreme weakening of the executive power in the interest of individual liberty by the introduction of the collegial executive. The outcome of these destabilizing influences in the Uruguayan case took, at the end of 1966, the form of the readoption of the uninomial executive, thus strengthening the government's ability to carry through a retrenchment in consumption standards for a temporary period and a general economic reorganization. The availability of this standing alternative made it possible to reject the existing political forms without going outside the constitutional-democratic tradition, however.

Destabilizing effects may also result from changes in the range of groups participating in the society, and thus in the structure of the relations among political forces, which may still derive from migration or from technological changes. The possible destabilizing effects deriving from migration are visible in several of the democratic polities today, as their egalitarian premises are being put to strain by an influx of people from less-developed societies, usually of darker skin color, who are thus not self-evidently acceptable to the masses as equals. This is occurring with respect to the migration of Southern Negroes into the northern United States, of Africans, West Indians, Indians, and Pakistanis into the United Kingdom, to some extent of Portuguese and Algerians into France, and of southern Italians, Turks, and Spaniards into West Germany and Switzerland. The political system can maintain its egalitarian premises in the face of such immigration by either of two techniques: by refusing to make distinctions between new immigrants and established residents, which is on the whole the line of action followed in France and, albeit with much travail, in the northern United States; or on some specious but nominally nonracial grounds to restrict the inflow—the method being followed by the British.[7]

The group structure of the developed societies will inevitably continue to change, in addition, under the impact of technological change that results in the creation of new classes and subclasses. As a rule the open and egalitarian nature of the modern democratic state makes it possible for newly emergent classes to be absorbed smoothly into the political system, however. Thus, in a multiparty system new parties tend to develop to reflect the interests of newly emergent groups—as the Christian Democrats of Latin America seem to be making themselves the spokesmen for new "technocratic" elements—without altering the basic political processes of the system. In a two-party system, both parties, or at least the weaker of the two major parties, will focus on the interests of newly participating groups as part of the continual modification of the party "image" that two-party competition requires; thus the British Labour party under Harold Wilson has been attempting to recruit emergent technocratic elements in Britain. It is possible that drastic technological change might have seriously destabilizing political effects, for example by producing a large class of permanent unemployables. This possibility is unlikely to occur, for many reasons, but is cited here to show that the modern democratic state, although relatively highly stable, can nevertheless not be assumed to represent an absolute final stage of political evolution for the present era.

As was noted in the previous chapter, there are several roads which lead to political stability in a democratic era. This is as much as to say that the specific processes of development do not consist simply of steady quantitative rises in indicators of development, reflecting a homogeneous and simply cumulative process. On the contrary, political development is characteristically uneven, attainment with respect to one aspect of development outrunning attainment in other respects, with inconsistencies, bottlenecks, and archaisms remaining unresolved and even persisting as minor themes when the country can be said to be on the whole developed.[8]

In view of this, it is an oversimplification to regard political development as a matter of cumulative advance in a single *formal* process, for example that of institution building, as Huntington does.[9] The substantive content of the process of development—in the current era, participation on terms of equality—cannot be overlooked. Thus for certain phases of the development process, with respect to certain areas of social and political life, the problem is certainly that of institution building; at other stages and in other areas it may equally be that of the destruction of institutions, or their drastic modification.

This can clearly be seen in the case of Latin America. Since the central characteristic of the developed polity is the theme of equality, the different forms of the structural resistance to political development will depend in each society on the character of the inequalities which it embodies. For Latin American countries, as pointed out above, these are summarized in the country's socioracial structure. The traditional Indian countries, for example, are rich in institutions which must be destroyed before development can take place: a web of feudal rights in the countryside, an entrenched pattern of elite dominance, powerful regional and particularistic loyalties. Even the strength of political parties and a functioning party system, which Huntington regards as a key to political development —a correct view as regards the later stages of the development process—can nevertheless be highly dysfunctional for development in the earlier stages. This can be seen if one considers the relation to development of the deeply entrenched two-party systems in Colombia, Nicaragua, Honduras, and Paraguay. In these countries, as was pointed out above, strong party identification has the character of the polarization of opinion in preparation for combat, rather than preparing the way for the peaceful competition for the allegiance of the center of the political spectrum characteristic of two-party systems in developed countries. In the latter cases, the dynamics of party competition reinforce the moderate leadership in both parties; where party rivalry reaches the extremes of combat or preparation for combat, on the other hand, extremist leadership is strengthened.

The fact that Chile has advanced further politically than other mestizo countries may be traced to the supersession of the traditional conflict between Conservative and

Liberal oligarchies by economic and demographic factors which have no counterpart in the other mestizo countries. In Chile the importance of mining and commerce blurred the distinction between a landowning Conservative class and a class of Liberal professionals. The concentration of the population in the central portion of the country around Santiago created no counterpart to the intercity rivalries between Granada and León in Nicaragua, between Tegucigalpa and San Pedro Sula in Honduras, or among Bogotá, Medellín, and Cali in Colombia. In Chile, moreover, the range of social classes and subclasses claiming representation in the political system was expanded by extensive European immigration. This, together with the greater importance of mining, provided the basis for a party structure broader than the Liberal-Conservative dichotomy: the mines, in Chile as elsewhere fostering a highly alienated and radical work force, provided the basis for a Communist party; small farmers, workers, lower professionals, and public servants of European antecedents provided the basis for the Socialist party, while the better-off and better-established elements of the same groups contributed its core to the Radical party. Given this political spectrum, the balance of political power drifted outside the Conservative-Liberal framework, first to the Radicals, and more recently to the new Christian Democratic party. The older sociopolitical structure has not been broken up, but the conflicts within it have subsided, it has diminished in relative importance, and it thus does not constitute an absolute impediment to social and political change.

It can thus be argued that the Latin American countries with the lowest degree of institutionalization and the most fluid social and political structures are the most likely prospects to attain a new equilibrium increasingly embodying the norms of equality and individual autonomy. In terms of the typology developed in Chapter Six, these are the Spanish-speaking mulatto countries. This may be especially clear in the cases of Venezuela and Panama, but the author is inclined to go further and rate the prospect of even the apparently hopeless cases of Cuba and the

Dominican Republic as better than those of Ecuador, Peru, and Guatemala or of Nicaragua, Honduras, and Paraguay. Clearly Cuba and the Dominican Republic do not seem likely prospects for development in a democratic sense at the present time. The many conditions working in Cuba's favor have not been taken advantage of, as Fidel Castro's immaturity became sectarian extremism, resulting in a political system of exclusion instead of inclusion, of polarization instead of emerging consensus. This in turn opened up the prospect that for a generation to come Cuban development will be marked by setbacks rather than advances.

In the Dominican Republic, the American intervention of 1965 has rescued, at least temporarily, the "estate" of self-seeking military officers who constitute the principal obstacle to social and institutional change. At the time of writing, this had not yet completely destroyed all basis for a consensus that could permit a beginning to be made on the continuing construction of democratic institutions, although it greatly undermined the strength of the evolutionary alternative and considerably enhanced the appeal of the revolutionary left for the younger generation. In Venezuela and Panama, the favorable conditions for development have long been obscured by political turmoil and major economic problems, but the long-term forces working for development are becoming clearer as the chances of economic disaster recede, as the influence of the military gradually diminishes, and as the party systems crystallize and the parties acquire continuing identity.

At first glance, evolutionary change seems hardly possible in the "traditional" Indian countries—Peru, Ecuador, and Guatemala. The social rigidities appear too great, the dominant classes appear too well entrenched, the social distance between whites and Indians appears too wide. Economic and technical changes which have developmental effects elsewhere may in these countries merely be used by the dominant classes to reinforce the present social and political order. Thus rises of productivity in the modern sector of the economy may only serve to widen the gap between it and the traditional subsistence sector. Road building and air transport facilities may only serve to move troops more quickly to crush Indian uprisings. And as anthropologists have pointed out, not only the "white" sector of the society utilizes newly available resources to strengthen the status quo, but so do traditional leadership elements within the Indian communities.

It should however be noted that not all forces work in the direction of the reinforcement of the status quo and that over the very long run political development may be possible even in these societies. It is always possible, of course, that conflict generated by events occurring in another context may have the effect of mobilizing the Indian populations and shaking them loose from traditional ways, as occurred in Mexico and Bolivia. It is also conceivable that in the very long run the traditional feudal order, while continuing to exist, will involve proportionately fewer and fewer of the national population while an ever-increasing proportion will be involved with the modern sector, which will then provide the dominant themes of national life.

Developments in Ecuador suggest at least a possibility of this eventual outcome. The Ecuadorean coastal provinces used to be very sparsely inhabited, because of the prevalence of tropical diseases. Since these were wiped out by modern public health measures and internal migration was made more feasible by the building of the railroads, the population of the coast has grown very rapidly in what can be thought of as empty social space, so that today the port of Guayaquil has a larger population than Quito, the capital of the country, and more of the national population lives on the coast than in the sierra. The social structure of Guayaquil is of course much more fluid and egalitarian than that of the sierra; the economic character and political attitudes of the port city are also quite different from those prevailing in the highlands and give rise to economic, political, and quasi-racial enmity between Quito and Guayaquil. For the traditional sociopolitical structure of Ecuador to be modified altogether by evolutionary demographic change of this type would take many generations, and it is difficult to see how similar changes could take place in Guatemala. Nevertheless, the possibility must be raised, to indicate that even in the most traditional Latin American countries the pattern of future development cannot be construed so as to eliminate evolutionary change completely from consideration.

It was argued in Chapter Five that political development accompanies economic development. On the whole, in those countries which are developed both politically and economically the two orders continue to reinforce each other. A stable political order with constitutional restraints on arbitrary government action helps to create a relatively secure environment in which economic activity can go forward and investment decisions can be made with confidence. Relative satisfaction with a productive economic order reinforces contentment with the political scheme of things, while the high economic levels provide a technical basis, in communications media and educational standards, for more sophisticated and effective exercise of the suffrage and operation of the institutions of government. The mutuality of these relations of influence should be noted; while it would be correct to say that economic development helps to contribute to political development, and vice versa, it would not be correct to say that either process must have been initiated before the other can begin.

While the net tendency is in the direction of mutual reinforcement, this is not always clear in the short run.[10] For example, one of the ways in which an economy can be developed is along Stalinist lines, that is, through the forced accumulation of capital and coercive central planning; in the political order this is clearly accompanied logically by the repression of dissent and the reduction of individual autonomy.[11] As the post-Stalin evolution in the Soviet Union demonstrates, however, the attainment of a relatively developed economy seems to be accompanied not only by pressures for an increase in consumption, but also by the reduction of coercion and arbitrariness in the political system.

This phenomenon has its counterpart when the requirements of political development are placed first. Rapid
political development in the dimensions of equality and
participation may entail a short-run setback for the cause
of economic development in the form of a loss of production discipline (as has been apparent in the Bolivian mining industry since the revolution of 1952) and a disruption
of those processes of production which are closely related
to the system of social ordination; for example, agricultural
production under a system of large estates.

Similarly, the direction of long-term political trends may
not be clear, and "phase changes" in political processes may
appear to take place dialectically rather than smoothly
and homogeneously, obscuring the long-term tendencies
at work. Thus the rapid expansion of political participation that has accompanied accelerated economic growth
in Venezuela, while it has made possible the attainment
of a stable state of political development at some future
time, has meanwhile been expressed in a high order of
turbulence and violence. As was pointed out in Chapter
Five, in the short run political participation is expanded
at the expense of political stability.

Although it is possible to discuss the compatibility of
economic and political development in terms of their direct
interrelations, there is an interesting, indeed intriguing,
sense in which both economic and political development
may be regarded as dependent variables each heavily influ-
enced by a third order of reality. This point is distinct
from the socioracial thesis advanced in Chapter Six, which
attempted to account for the fact that in some countries a
higher order of political development was expressed in
greater political stability, while in others it took the form
of wider participation. We are now asking why some
countries are more developed—in any sense—than others.

At different states of technology, economic development
is based on different types of available resources. During
the colonial period Mexico and Peru might have been
considered "economically developed" countries, since they

were rich in the resources important under the technological conditions of the period—mines of precious metals
and large quantities of exploitable labor. Because of their
lack of these resources, countries which today are regarded
as fairly well developed, such as Argentina, Uruguay, and
Costa Rica, were then wasteland or miserable frontier out-
posts. Today, however, the resources most important for
economic development, as economists are coming to appreciate, are human resources.[12] With the exception of oil,
the resources possessed by the wealthier countries, in Latin
America and elsewhere, are primarily the resources of an
educated, skilled, and well-organized population.

To the extent that economic and political development
do go hand in hand today, it is therefore likely that a major causal factor working in both dimensions lies in quali-
ties of the country's population. It has long been a persistent theme in the literature that the character of certain
population elements is particularly favorable for political
development. The stress continually given to the compatibility of a stable constitutional order with the presence of
a large middle class, for example, derives partly from assumptions about the relations of class structure to political
structure, but is also based on hypotheses about the presence of various favorable skills and attitudes among the
middle class.

In analyzing critically theories that stress the importance
of a strong middle class, one should first note that in most
countries today, the "middle" class is not a "middle class."
The extraordinary linguistic confusion which surrounds this
point clearly represents a hangover from a previous era
in which the hereditary aristocracy was still a political factor of importance. Today the so-called "middle class," that
is, the bourgeoisie, is clearly high into the upper half of the
socioeconomic structure of any country except perhaps a
handful of very traditional South Asian and Near Eastern
monarchies. In Latin America today, certainly, the classes
genuinely "in the middle" of the social structure are
organized labor, small property-holding farmers, and white
collar workers—as distinct from the relatively well-to-do

businessmen whom sociologists usually think of as the "middle class," on one side, and, on the other, the marginally employed urban poor and landless agricultural laborers.[13]

If one thinks in terms of human skills and attitudes, rather than of social structure per se, one is reminded of the conclusions of the voting studies that political participation is a function of the individual's sense of personal efficacy, to use the happy phrase coined by the authors of *The American Voter,* and that sense of efficacy, like political participation itself, increases with higher socioeconomic status. The available evidence is thus compatible with the notion that the presence of a large middle class provides the social base for a participatory polity because heightened objective social status leads to heightened subjective self-respect, which in turn provides the psychological basis for political participation. Put in these terms, this conclusion converges with those of studies ostensibly on other subjects. Thus Crane Brinton's conclusion, now widely accepted, that revolutions occur when a group's improved social and economic position is not accompanied by increased political power can be translated into terms of a heightened sense of efficacy, deriving from improvement in social and economic status, which leads to a participant orientation that cannot be accommodated within the existing political order.[14]

This subjective psychological factor of heightened self-respect, leading to heightened sense of efficacy, can also be seen at work in other sets of circumstances. We are commonly told, for example, that the developing countries of today are in the grip of "rising expectations." The usual reasons adduced for the development of rising expectations are along the lines of a demonstration effect: it is argued that, for the first time, due to improved communications and so on, the deprived are becoming aware that others live at higher levels than they do. On reflection, however, it can be seen that this explanation is patently false. The deprived have always known that others lived at higher levels than they; in virtually all societies except the most

primitive there are ruling classes disposing of a dispropor-
tionate share of the national resources, and very often a
lower class of agricultural workers is in continual contact
with members of the possessing classes who act in super-
visory roles. The new factor in the situation which creates
rising expectations is not the demonstration that a higher
standard of living is possible, but rather a growing belief
on the part of the deprived that they are *entitled* to such
a higher standard. In other words, the new factor is a
heightened self-respect.

The revolutionary effect of heightened self-respect can
be seen in many sets of political circumstances. At the root
of the current racial upheaval in the American South, for
example, as of the anticolonial revolution in Africa, is the
gradual, slow, and fitful abandonment by the Negro of his
acceptance of the idea that he is inferior to the white. It
should be added that the revolutionary effects of heightened feelings of self-assurance may operate in other than
pro-democratic directions: a similar factor seems to be
present in the initiation of imperialist policies.

In this perspective, economic development can be regarded as one among several ways of producing heightened
self-assurance (by raising living standards, or merely by
breaking the rigidity of a socioeconomic structure premised
on the average person's low social worth). Other ways of
increasing self-assurance are indoctrination in new ideas or
mobilization into combat, Bolivian or Mexican style.

Although this conclusion suggests that attitude change
plays a role in political development, it should not be assumed that attitude change of this order presupposes a
change in basic personality. Here the author parts company with Everett Hagen, who has written: "The inter-
relationships between personality and social structure are
such as to make it clear that social change will not occur
without change in personalities." [15]

Although he finds himself in agreement with much
that Dr. Hagen writes in his virtuoso synthesis of insights
drawn from the various social sciences in the attempt to
understand the process of social change, the writer does

not consider it necessary or even appropriate to explain
attitude change of this type by reference to the dynamics
of individual personality structures in the psychoanalytic
sense. Discussion of these factors is not necessary because
at certain levels of understanding the internal personality
dynamics of the persons involved may be disregarded
(individual personality may be regarded as a "black box").
Similar politically relevant attitudes and behaviors can be
exhibited in similar situations by individuals possessing
totally different personality structures. This phenomenon
is due to two factors. First, situational imperatives may be
so exigent that certain behaviors become mandatory regardless of individual preferences. Second, a common set of
politically relevant attitudes and behaviors may be shared
by people with totally different personality structures because such attitudes and behaviors perform quite different
functions in the economy of the different personalities.[16]
For example, an individual in a noncommunist country
might become a communist because: (1) in rebelling
against a brutal and inconsistent father who represents
authority to him, he chooses the most revolutionary creed
in the political spectrum; (2) he has a strong need to
identify with a beloved father or father-figure of extreme
radical views; (3) he has a strong need to achieve, yet is
born into a working-class family in a rigid social structure,
so that the only leadership positions available to him are
within the labor movement, and the competition for leadership positions within the movement determines that victory goes to the politically most radical; (4) political opinions are of low salience to him, and he unthinkingly
accepts the radical political views of his family or workmates in order to minimize social friction. A host of other
sets of circumstances can be imagined in which individuals
with totally different personality needs nevertheless arrive
at the same political attitudes and behaviors. Fortunately,
however, it is possible at some levels of analysis to short-
circuit the personality question entirely in handling cause-
effect relations, even though those relations are of course
mediated in some way through the personality structure.[17]

Thus, studies of voting behavior indicate that for some purposes of gross aggregate analysis party affiliation is predictable on the basis of such "social facts" as the affiliations of family members and workmates, regardless of the specific nature of the psychodynamic modes by which the influence of such social facts becomes registered on individual behavior.

It should further be noted that when the stress is placed exclusively on psychodynamic processes as the originators of changes in behavior it becomes impossible to understand how major social changes can take place over shorter time periods than at least one generation, since change in the environment, in Hagen's approach, needs to be translated into change in the basic personality through alterations in child-rearing practices. It appears to be true, however, that changes in politically relevant attitudes and behaviors may take place purely in response to situational or environmental changes, without any change in the basic personality's being presumed. For example, the leader of a potentially imperialist state may be deterred from overt imperialist behavior by the construction of a countervailing coalition; it is not necessary to account for his change to less aggressive behavior by resorting to the hypothesis of a change in personality structure which reduces the personality need for aggression.

It is thus possible to explain a change in political behavior by reference to heightened feelings of self-assurance, as has been done above, without implying that change in basic personality structure has taken place. Such change may well take place in some cases; but it need not invariably be assumed.

As "social mobilization" takes place, then, usually (but not always and not necessarily) under the stimulus of economic change, people become more self-assured and more prone to participate in politics. Inkeles' (as yet unpublished) attitude survey data from Chile and Argentina indicate that feelings of political efficacy, the propensity to participate in politics, and faith in democracy all rise with indices of modernization and with higher education levels. This might well have been expected and confirms Almond's and Verba's findings from the five countries they surveyed.[18]

As was pointed out in Chapter Five, however, Lipset and Inkeles also found that the tendency to accept the existing political system declined as these indicators rose. In the "developing" countries of Latin America, the situation thus arises—hypothesized in Chapter One—of a tension between democratic aspirations and an alienation from existing political practices which is not only subjective but also has an objective basis in the contrast between the formally enjoined norms of the constitutional order and the realities of informal political processes. Evidence for the existence of this tension from Almond's and Verba's Mexican data and Goldrich's data from Panama was pointed out in Chapter One. It has already been suggested (in Chapter Five) that this inverse correlation between propensity to participate and support for the existing state of things provides the psychological basis for the inverse correlation between the two dimensions of democratic political development, participation and constitutional stability.

In Latin America (again, generalizing and thus oversimplifying) the contradiction between democratic norms and nondemocratic realities has always existed, giving rise to the familiar "legitimacy vacuum" and the resulting political turbulence. The new element in the situation, then, is a heightened sense of efficacy, and thus will to participate, on the part of the masses. The entry of the masses as an active element in the political arena introduces a tendency to political development and the long-run transformation of the political system which becomes visible even through the oscillations of the state of "permanent instability," as was pointed out in Chapter Two. The formal democratic norms of the system are thus given new life as the aspirations of the increasingly vocal masses. The tension between the heightened self-assurance of the mobilized masses and the traditional social and political structure which frustrates their aspirations creates a classic revolutionary situation, signaling the final breakdown of the old order.

VI
Conclusion

The major empirical generalizations made throughout the book can now be integrated and presented in the following set of theorems.

1. At any one time a limited number of political ideas are generally acceptable as the basis for a country's formal institutions and government policies. Today the dominant set of ideas is that of "democracy."

2. A system of government remains stable when it reflects the informal distribution of power, when its policies gratify the needs of those subject to it, or when they accept the validity of its ideological bases.

3. When a change occurs in one of the components of the polity, an inherent tendency to consistency normally causes the change either to be rejected or else to modify other components of the polity into harmony with it. If both the element embodying the change and some other component of the polity strongly resist modification, then a condition of "permanent instability" can be created in which mutually inconsistent behaviors are enjoined for individuals. Such a condition may last for a considerable time before one element becomes dominant and the polity begins to "evolve" in the direction of a new stability.

4. With the exception of a period of stability based on a favorable configuration of economic and ideological conditions prevailing around the beginning of the twentieth century, independent Latin America has generally been "permanently unstable" as a result of the tension between sets of formal institutions based on democratic and egalitarian premises, on the one hand, and informal institutions based on radically inegalitarian premises, on the other.

This dichotomy created not only two sets of political behaviors, but also a third, deriving from the cynicism growing out of perception of this dichotomy and thus characterized by lack of moral restraints, based on opportunism, peculation, and reliance on naked force.

5. The patterns of permanent instability express themselves in three types of purposive political violence: "supplantive violence," the replacement of one ruling group by another representing a similar configuration of social forces, and with minimal or no policy significance; "representational violence," which seeks to secure the gratification of limited demands by the threat implicit in their public dramatization; and the "good government" revolution, which aims at the reestablishment of fidelity to legal and constitutional norms.

6. Other types of revolution are characteristic not of the processes of permanent instability but of the shift from systemic instability to systemic evolution and aim at the modernization of administrative and fiscal structures; at the democratization of the political system; or at the transformation of the social and economic system in the interest of the disadvantaged.

7. Revolutionary social innovation is distinguished by its rejection of the inhibitions to rapid social change imposed by preexisting legal and constitutional norms. Revolutionary modes of change are prone to prove costly and, in the short run, counterproductive.

8. Evolutionary social innovation may aim at far-reaching changes but accepts the restraints of preexisting constitutional and legal codes. It may prove extremely slow or even totally ineffectual unless a skilled leadership can take advantage of favorable opportunities provided by the structure of the distribution of political power.

9. Most recently there have been various signs that the pattern of permanent instability has started to give way in Latin America as the tendency to evolution toward stable systems based on democratic premises has gradually begun to assert itself.

10. Institutions characteristic of a polity evolving toward stable democracy—for example, the "democratic single

party"—may be functional for the process of evolution while themselves not fully democratic in character. Similarly, institutions appropriate to a developed democratic polity may not be functional for one that is evolving.

11. As a country develops economically, it also develops politically.

12. Economic development promotes political development in several ways, a principal way being through the fostering of heightened feelings of self-assurance. In some cases such feelings can arise from noneconomic causes, such as participation in combat; but whatever their origin, they still make possible a higher level of political development.

13. Political development in a democratic era has two aspects: a greater obedience to constitutional norms and the expansion of the proportion of the population participating in politics. Any measurement of political development must take both of these dimensions into account.

14. Political development may express itself by advances in one of these dimensions rather than the other. The common tendency is for political development to express itself first in higher participation where the social structure is more egalitarian and in higher fidelity to constitutional norms where the social structure is more hierarchic.

15. In Latin America, the chief characteristic determining the degree of equality reflected in a country's informal economic and political institutions is the distribution of the population into "racial" groups, as these are socially and culturally defined.

16. For any given level of economic development in the range between stable nondevelopment and relatively complete development, *but not beyond either limit,* constitutional stability and the extent of participation in politics appear to be in inverse relation to each other. For example, at any given economic level within this range constitutional stability will be greater the more apathetic the population.

17. If the population has a high propensity to participate, then constitutional stability depends on the performance of the system in generating higher levels of income.

That is, as participation rises, constitutional stability will decline unless economic welfare rises also; alternatively, if participation remains constant, then constitutional stability will deteriorate if economic conditions deteriorate.

18. As mass participation has increased in Latin America in recent years, resistance to it has mounted, taking the form of military intervention.

19. Although the social and professional characteristics of the armed forces have developed in ways paralleling changes taking place elsewhere in society, the fact that the military have acted politically so as to attempt to frustrate these changes rather than reinforce them indicates that military intervention is "pulled" by extramilitary forces rather than "pushed" by intramilitary ones; it is thus primarily a function of the behavior of the total political system.

20. When mass participation rises faster than economic levels, the resultant deterioration in constitutional functioning takes the form of representational violence, that is, violence in support of unsatisfied demands directed against the government, which always retains the possibility of becoming revolutionary violence.

21. A dictatorship can arise in a mass participation society, but it can perpetuate itself only by becoming totalitarian, that is, by incorporating into its functioning a channeled and controlled mass participation.

22. In a developing society, mass politicization increases even under a dictatorship. This shows itself in a high propensity to participate after the death or removal of the dictator.

23. Various political and public-policy characteristics of the modern democratic state suggest that, although the emergence of certain specific destabilizing forces is possible, the strongest tendencies are for it to remain in stable equilibrium.

The results of the analysis have given the author no reason to regret an approach to the subject that declined at the outset to accept philosophies of history which lay stress on one type of determinant to the exclusion of others. It still seems reasonable to suppose that an intellectual controversy can endure only where there is some truth on both sides of the argument. Perhaps it is worthwhile making this point explicit by reviewing the material presented here in the light of three philosophical and, in a general sense, methodological, antinomies.

Idealism Versus Materialism

The importance of material factors has been pointed out throughout; and the general conclusion that political development accompanies economic development may come too close to economic determinism for the taste of many readers. Yet at the same time the key significance of the ideological factor in assuring or undermining stability has been stressed, almost to the point of Hegelianism, in Chapters One and Two, and again in Chapters Seven and Eight.

The Psychological Versus the Sociological

While the explanatory power of situational determinants external to the individual has most frequently been relied on, especially in the discussion of military intervention in Chapter Four, the role of psychological factors has been acknowledged in Chapters One and Three and to some extent in Chapter Eight.

Impersonal Forces Versus the Autonomy of Individuals

In a general discussion conducted on the level of analysis used here, the stress necessarily has to be on the trans-individual determinants of social processes. At the same time, the impact of autonomous individual decisions has been pointed out in Chapter Two and, especially in relation to strategic choices, in Chapter Seven.

It remains true that on the whole the burden of explanation has been laid on impersonal forces and situational determinants, especially those of an economic character. Thus in the approach taken here the broad tendencies of Latin American history can be regarded as deriving from either continuing or newly relevant configurations of forces of this type, represented schematically as follows:

1. The geographic characteristics of the different regions of Latin America, as these were given significance by the conceptions of economic value, the nature of world trade, and the technological level of the period of the Conquest and the colonial era, determined the original patterns of settlement. Thus it was determined that Indians would work in mines and Negroes on sugar plantations and subsequently that Argentina and Uruguay would have pastoral economies, European populations, and high income levels.

2. In this way the regional ecologies of Latin America were established, giving rise in turn[1] to the distinctive social structures and the typical behavior patterns of each region. Within these social structures, there also persisted elements originating in the ecologies of the Old World that had become imbedded in the cultural patterns of the immigrants, such as the transplanting to Costa Rica of the Basque tradition of the family farm, which the Basque regions shared in common with other relatively high rainfall areas of Spain.[2]

3. The social structures deriving from these ecological relationships are in turn reflected in the systems of parties and pressure groups that constitute the balance of sociopolitical forces and that determine the directions which subsequent change can take and the political strategies which are feasible.

4. At the same time, changes in economic levels resulting from changes in the value a country's resources are given by changing patterns of world trade and changing technologies provide politics with its issues, policy with its resources, and government with its popular support or lack of it.

At each level, autonomous areas for individual decision

remain. But the major parameters of the situation within which the individual must act can only be treated by him as given; and the values at whose maximization his actions aim are predominantly derived from his situation as a member of a given type of family, of a specific social class, and of a determinate culture area. It is after all this fundamental truth that makes the social sciences possible.

Notes

Introduction

1. The writer has discussed this question in "On the Dangers of Copying from the British," *Political Science Quarterly* (Spring 1962).

2. It is clear that many countries of Latin America are still striving to attain the purely formal objectives which any political order seeks, that is, simply to be a regularly functioning system of some kind consistent with its own premises. As Federico Gil has put it: "Unfortunately, perhaps, the problem of Latin America has been the primary one of getting along in an orderly or semi-orderly way under *any* political system" (emphasis in original). Comment on W. W. Pierson (ed.), "Pathology of Democracy in Latin America: A Symposium," *American Political Science Review* (March 1950), p. 149.

3. What is referred to here as "participation on terms of equality" seems to be the same dual characteristic discussed with greater exactitude by Frederick Frey as the "distribution and reciprocity of power." Higher participation, in my formulation, translates into Frey's terms as wider distribution and greater reciprocity of power. See his "Political Development, Power, and Communications in Turkey," in Lucian W. Pye (ed.), *Communications and Political Development* (Princeton, N.J.: Princeton University Press, 1963), p. 301.

4. For purposes of consistency and comparability, the attempt has been made to use data having reference to the situation in about 1960, except where an author's work which uses data from another period is being critically considered.

5. Perhaps the literature is too rich, the theses too brilliantly stated. The writer finds, to his embarrassment, much truth in R. P. Dore's observation that the students of Latin America have become too "Latin American"; Dore argues that they "are personalists, irresponsible, disorganized, ideological,

and preoccupied with demonstrating their *machismo*." "Latin America and Japan Compared," in John J. Johnson (ed.), *Continuity and Change in Latin America* (Stanford: Stanford University Press, 1964), p. 232.

6. Arthur Whitaker, "Pathology of Democracy in Latin America: A Historian's Point of View," *American Political Science Review* (March 1950), p. 117.

Chapter One

1. This formulation appears to have points of resemblance to that of John R. P. French and Bertram Raven, who approach the problem from a different direction. See "The Bases of Social Power," reprinted in J. David Singer (ed.), *Human Behavior and International Politics* (Chicago: Rand McNally, 1965), pp. 136–144. Compare also P. A. Brunt's discussion of the reasons for the acceptance of Roman rule by the Empire's non-Italian subjects in his "Reflections on British and Roman Imperialism," *Comparative Studies in Society and History* (April 1965), p. 269.

2. Pride of place goes of course to David Easton. See his *The Political System* (New York: Knopf, 1953); *A Framework for Political Analysis* (Englewood Cliffs, N.J.: Prentice-Hall, 1965); and especially *A Systems Analysis of Political Life* (New York: Wiley, 1965).

3. There are certainly boundary problems here, particularly in demarcating the informal system of dominance relations from the formal structure of public authority, which I do not wish to get into at this point. I do not believe, however, that any of the recent work done in political science which starts from a more general, "sociological" perspective, need be interpreted so as to weaken or eliminate the distinction made here between the formal structures of public authority and the parallel informal processes. As Pye writes in his introduction to *Communications and Political Development*, "First, the realm of politics, as generally thought of, consists of two rather different forms of activities, involving different structures. These are, on the one hand, the domain of administration and formal government and, on the other hand, the political processes of the society which permeate in a diffuse fashion the entire society and provide the fundamental framework of the polity." Lucian W. Pye (ed.), *Communications*

and Political Development (Princeton, N.J.: Princeton University Press, 1963), p. 16.

4. A particularly good discussion of the development of Chilean politics can be found in Federico Gil, *Genesis and Modernization of Political Parties in Chile* (Gainesville: University of Florida Press, 1962).

5. This formulation seems to the writer to have, among others, the merit that it makes it possible to talk about political evolution or political development without one's own predilections about which directions of change are desirable and which are not entering in.

6. The concept of permanent instability used here seems similar to that of unstable equilibrium developed in John S. Chipman, "The Nature and Meaning of Equilibrium in Economic Theory," in Don Martindale (ed.), *Functionalism in the Social Sciences* (Philadelphia: American Academy of Political and Social Science, 1965), pp. 51–53.

7. José Medina Echevarría regards the period of Conservative-Liberal rivalry of much of nineteenth-century Latin America as a stably functioning system, which seems to the present writer to stretch the concept of stability outside its normal range of meaning, including that of Medina's own definition, although the term "unstable equilibrium" might reasonably be used. See "A Sociologist's View" in J. Medina Echevarría and Benjamin Higgins, *Social Aspects of Economic Development in Latin America* (Paris: UNESCO, 1963), II, 84. In other respects, however, Medina's less formal approach stresses the same factors considered relevant to stability here: changes in the economic, demographic, ideological, and dominance dimensions. *Ibid.*, pp. 80, 81. His explicit definition of systemic stability also appears the same: Stability obtains where a system functions in accordance with its own political formula. *Ibid.*, p. 81.

8. *Ibid.*, p. 44. Since, as Seymour Martin Lipset has pointed out to the writer, this gap between ideology and reality is general and has been demonstrated by attitude data from the United States as well, the special character of this gap for the Latin American countries (and, presumably, for other countries at similar stages of development) lies not in the fact of its existence, but in its breadth. The point should thus be cast in the more exact form used by Gino Germani, who has written of the gap between constitutional prescription and social practice in Latin America: "But nowhere

was there a deeper gulf between reality and law." *Política y sociedad en una epoca de transición* (Buenos Aires: Editorial Paidos, 1962), p. 161.

9. Daniel Goldrich, "Toward an Estimate of the Probability of Social Revolutions in Latin America: Some Orienting Concepts and a Case Study," *The Centennial Review* (Summer 1962), p. 405.

10. *Ibid.*, p. 397.

11. Gabriel A. Almond and Sidney Verba, *The Civic Culture: Political Attitudes and Democracy in Five Nations* (Princeton, N.J.: Princeton University Press, 1963), p. 414.

12. *Ibid.*, p. 415. In other words, Mexicans believe themselves able to influence government decisions by political means, but they actually attempt to do so very infrequently.

13. This is, without exception, the view of all observers. It is impossible to cite all the sources in agreement with this statement.

14. The author believes cultural factors are also important here.

15. Regionalism, kinship, and *compadrazgo* (ritual godparent relations), for example. In nineteenth-century political combat in Mexico, conflicting loyalties were even based on membership in masonic lodges of either the Scottish or the Yorkist rite.

Chapter Two

1. Gino Germani has analyzed recent Argentine politics from this perspective: "In all the previous instances in Argentina, the attempt to establish a totalitarian state was doomed to failure. And this can be said also of the Peronist regime. The reasons for this failure must be sought in the social structure of Argentina and in the strong democratic tradition prevailing in the country. In fact, one of the Argentine paradoxes is the fact that while representative democracy does not function—at least in the last 36 years—its ideology is dominant in the population." Talk given in New York, December 5, 1966; cited in *Hemispherica* (December 1966), p. 3.

2. For an extended discussion of a typical case, see Martin C. Needler, *Anatomy of a Coup d'Etat: Ecuador, 1963* (Washington, D.C.: Institute for the Comparative Study of Political Systems, 1964), p. 30.

3. Without giving the actual figures, John J. Johnson has pointed out this tendency for military coups to eventuate

increasingly in juntas rather than individual rulers. "The Latin-American Military as a Politically Competing Group in Transitional Society," in John J. Johnson (ed.), *The Role of the Military in Underdeveloped Countries* (Princeton, N.J.: Princeton University Press, 1962), p. 119.

4. Similarly Joseph LaPalombara has generalized, on the basis of a series of essays and case studies which do not include any Latin American material, that "it would appear somewhat irrational to superimpose on any of the developing nations the principles and organizational characteristics of public administration that have evolved in the United States." "An Overview of Bureaucracy and Political Development," in Joseph LaPalombara (ed.), *Bureaucracy and Political Development* (Princeton, N.J.: Princeton University Press, 1963), p. 20.

5. C. Northcote Parkinson has lampooned these interviews very nicely in one of the chapters of *Parkinson's Law*, distinguishing between a "Chinese" examination system, whose criterion is ability, and a "British" system, whose criterion is social savoir-faire.

6. On the persistence of upper class domination of the higher military ranks in Britain, see Philip Abrams, "Democracy, Technology, and the Retired British Officer," in Samuel P. Huntington (ed.), *Changing Patterns of Military Politics* (New York: Free Press, 1962).

7. For a discussion of Vallenilla Lanz's opinions, see Leo B. Lott, "Venezuela," in Martin C. Needler (ed.), *Political Systems of Latin America* (Princeton, N.J.: Van Nostrand, 1964), p. 245.

8. José Medina Echevarría, "Relationships Between Social and Economic Institutions: A Theoretical Model Applicable to Latin America," *Economic Bulletin for Latin America* (March 1961), p. 30.

9. Edwin Lieuwen, *Arms and Politics in Latin America*, rev. ed. (New York: Praeger, 1961), p. 55.

10. Samuel P. Huntington, "Political Development and Political Decay," *World Politics* (April 1965), p. 408.

11. Lewis Hanke, *Modern Latin America: Continent in Ferment*, Vol. I: *Mexico and the Caribbean* (Princeton, N.J.: Van Nostrand, 1959), pp. 70–71.

12. Howard F. Cline, *The United States and Mexico*, rev. ed. (New York: Atheneum, 1963), p. 52.

13. *Ibid.*, p. 55.

14. More strictly speaking, the Ateneo had existed in an earlier incarnation, the Sociedad de Conferencias, beginning in 1907. Pedro Henríquez Ureña, *A Concise History of Latin American Culture*, Gilbert Chase (tr.) (New York: Praeger, 1966; first printing, 1947), p. 103. Henríquez Ureña was himself a founding member of the Ateneo.

15. An extended discussion can be found in Patrick Romanell, *The Making of the Mexican Mind* (Lincoln: University of Nebraska Press, 1952), Chap. 2.

16. Arthur Whitaker cites the conclusion of Leopoldo Zea that positivism "held as dominant a position in Latin American thought from the mid-nineteenth to the early twentieth century as scholasticism had held there during the colonial period." "Pathology of Democracy in Latin America: A Historian's Point of View," *American Political Science Review* (March 1950), p. 105.

17. The racist character of the immigration policy is pointed out by Gino Germani in *Política y sociedad en una epoca de transición* (Buenos Aires: Editorial Paidos, 1962), pp. 220–221.

18. Scobie writes: "By 1910 three out of every four adults in the city of Buenos Aires were European-born." James R. Scobie, *Argentina: A City and a Nation* (New York: Oxford University Press, 1964), p. 134. Germani, and Whitaker following Germani, both use the figure of 49 percent foreign-born for Greater Buenos Aires in 1914. Gino Germani, "The Transition to a Mass Democracy in Argentina," in Dwight B. Heath and Richard N. Adams (eds.), *Contemporary Cultures and Societies of Latin America* (New York: Random House, 1965), p. 461; Arthur P. Whitaker, *Argentina* (Englewood Cliffs, N.J.: Prentice-Hall, 1964), pp. 56–57.

19. One sociological study has gone so far as to take membership in the Sociedad Rural as one of the defining characteristics of the *urban* upper class. José Luis de Imaz, *La clase alta de Buenos Aires* (Buenos Aires: Instituto de Sociología de la Universidad de Buenos Aires, 1962).

20. Germani gives the percentages of foreign-born in some occupational categories in 1914 as entrepreneurs in industry, 66 percent; in commerce and services, 74 percent; professionals, 45 percent; industrial workers, 50 percent; domestic servants, 38 percent; laborers in domestic and craft industries, 27 percent. "The Transition to a Mass Democracy in Argentina," *op. cit.*, p. 465.

21. Scobie, *op. cit.*, p. 226.

22. Germani, "The Transition to a Mass Democracy in Argentina," *op. cit.*, p. 469.

23. Fredrick B. Pike, "Aspects of Class Relations in Chile 1850–1960," *Hispanic American Historical Review* (February 1963), p. 22.

24. *Ibid.*, p. 16.

25. A leading exponent of this latter view is John J. Johnson. See *The Military and Society in Latin America* (Stanford: Stanford University Press, 1964), especially pp. 3, 10, and 261–262.

26. Tad Szulc, *Twilight of the Tyrants* (New York: Holt, Rinehart and Winston, 1959).

27. Edwin Lieuwen, *Generals vs. Presidents* (New York: Praeger, 1964).

28. The idea of approaching the problem in this fashion was suggested to the author by Ronald Schneider's article "The U.S. in Latin America," *Current History* (January 1965). This appears to vindicate the position taken by Edwin Lieuwen that "although there have been short-term cyclical undulations in the pattern of military as opposed to civilian rule, the long-term secular trend is away from the former and is moving toward civilian government." Edwin Lieuwen, *Arms and Politics in Latin America*, rev. ed. (New York: Praeger, 1961), p. 171.

29. To be considered "dictatorial," a government (1) could not be an avowedly provisional regime holding office for thirty-six months or less; (2) had to come to power, or remain in power after the conclusion of the constitutionally prescribed term of office, by means other than a free and competitive election; or rule in clear disregard of constitutionally guaranteed liberties.

Chapter Three

1. William S. Stokes, "Violence as a Power Factor in Latin American Politics," *Western Political Quarterly* (September 1952).

2. Kalman H. Silvert, *The Conflict Society: Reaction and Revolution in Latin America* (New Orleans: Hauser Press, 1961), pp. 19–23.

3. Martin C. Needler, *Latin American Politics in Perspective* (Princeton, N.J.: Van Nostrand, 1963), pp. 78–82.

4. Sometimes the strictly societal and the social-psychological determinants are fused in a "national character" or "cultural character" approach. However, they are analytically distinct and should be kept methodologically separate. This problem is discussed in Emily M. Nett, "An Evaluation of the National Character Concept in Sociological Theory," reprinted from *Social Forces* in J. David Singer (ed.), *Human Behavior and International Politics* (Chicago: Rand McNally, 1965).

5. The term "Hispanic" is used consciously here to exclude Portuguese Brazil, whose tradition is clearly less violent. The question of how violent Brazilian politics is, compared with the Spanish-speaking countries, is discussed by James L. Busey in "Brazil's Reputation for Political Stability," *Western Political Quarterly* (December 1965). See the sources cited by Busey in the footnote to page 866 for agreement with the premise that Brazilian politics has been less violent.

6. This factor is stressed by William S. Stokes, for example. See his *Latin American Politics* (New York: Crowell, 1959), p. 107.

7. Cecil Jane, *Liberty and Despotism in Spanish America* (London: Clarendon, 1929).

8. See Frank Tannenbaum, *Ten Keys to Latin America* (New York: Knopf, 1963), pp. 75–76; John J. Johnson, *The Military and Society in Latin America* (Stanford: Stanford University Press, 1964), pp. 41–42; and Charles Wolf, Jr., "The Political Effects of Economic Programs: Some Indicators from Latin America," *Economic Development and Cultural Change* (October 1965), p. 18. The present writer has found no correlation between population size (which also roughly reflects geographic area) and "democratic" character as measured by the constitutionality index described in Chapter Five.

9. See, for example, the strained interpretation of the 1961 overthrow of Velasco Ibarra by Manuel Agustín Aguirre, reprinted from the *Monthly Review* as "Report from Ecuador" in Carlos Fuentes, *et al.*, *Whither Latin America?* (New York: Monthly Review Press, 1963), pp. 120–124.

10. Merle Kling, "Toward a Theory of Power and Political Instability in Latin America," *Western Political Quarterly* (March 1956). Kenneth F. Johnson has drawn on Kling's work in his "Causal Factors in Latin American Political Instability," *Western Political Quarterly* (September 1964). A comparable interpretation has been advanced in Eric R.

Wolf and Edward C. Hansen, "*Caudillo* Politics: A Structural Analysis," *Comparative Studies in Society and History* (January 1967).

11. Lucian Pye has pointed out that this is characteristic of all of the developing countries; he refers to it as a lack of political "brokers." See his "The Non-Western Political Process," *Journal of Politics* (August 1958). Hélio Jaguaribe has made the same point: "Political underdevelopment is characterized by the absence of mechanisms and processes able to guarantee representation, in the broad sense of the term, to social interests and expectations." *Desenvolvimento econômico e desenvolvimento político* (Rio de Janeiro: Editora Fundo de Cultura, 1962), p. 78.

12. Frank Tannenbaum, "Personal Government in Mexico," *Foreign Affairs* (October 1948).

13. As described in the *Hispanic American Report* for September 1962.

14. This interpretation of the role of representational violence appears to parallel that of Charles W. Anderson, who treats it as central to the functioning of the Latin American political system. See his "Toward a Theory of Latin American Politics," Occasional Paper No. 2 (Nashville: Graduate Center for Latin American Politics, Vanderbilt University, February 1964). The model developed by James Payne in "Peru: The Politics of Structured Violence," *Journal of Politics* (August 1965), is more rigorous but less comprehensive. Thus Payne makes one of the premises of his interpretation of the pervasiveness of popular violence that the armed forces will intervene to remove the president if dissatisfaction, evinced by violence, becomes extremely intense and widespread. Yet violence remains effective in countries where military intervention is not to be expected, that is, in Chile and Mexico. The weakening of the president's prestige, his party's electoral prospects, and the impetus behind his legislative program if he fails to meet demands seems to make violence effective even without the prospect of military intervention, although the latter doubtless increases its effectiveness. At the same time, the role assigned to military intervention in Payne's formulation—to preserve domestic peace—is too narrow, even in the case of Peru; there are other significant grounds for military intervention, as this chapter and the next one endeavor to make clear.

15. The term "supplantive" is adapted from Samuel E. Finer,

The Man on Horseback (New York: Praeger, 1963), pp. 87 ff.

16. See Martin C. Needler, *Anatomy of a Coup d'Etat: Ecuador, 1963* (Washington, D.C.: Institute for the Comparative Study of Political Systems, 1964).

17. Donald M. Dozer, "Roots of Revolution in Latin America," *Foreign Affairs* (January 1949), reprinted in Asher N. Christensen (ed.), *The Evolution of Latin American Government* (New York: Holt, Rinehart and Winston, 1951), pp. 295–296. Kenneth F. Johnson appears to follow this view in writing of "varying degrees of intensity of political alienation" which may pass over a "threshold of criticality" and lead to political instability, *op. cit.*, p. 435.

18. Crane Brinton, *The Anatomy of Revolution* (Englewood Cliffs, N.J.: Prentice-Hall, 1952). For similar formulations, see James C. Davies, "Toward a Theory of Revolution," *American Sociological Review* (February 1962); and Gerrit Huizer, "Peasant Organizations in the Process of Modernization: The Latin American Experience," unpublished paper delivered at the Conference on Urbanization and Work in Modernizing Areas, St. Thomas, V.I., November 2–4, 1967.

19. This formulation appears corroborated by all kinds of evidence. Thus Pertti Pesonen finds that the upsurge in communist strength in woodland areas of northeastern Finland "seems to be a result of a sudden rise in the aspiration level, accompanied by structural restraints on social participation." "Studies on Finnish Political Behavior," in Austin Ranney (ed.), *Essays on the Behavioral Study of Politics* (Urbana: University of Illinois Press, 1962), p. 228.

20. Karl R. Popper, *The Poverty of Historicism* (Boston: Beacon Press, 1957), p. 62. I have paraphrased Popper's formulation.

21. Theodore Draper, *Castro's Revolution: Myths and Realities* (New York: Praeger, 1962), pp. 3–59.

22. Calculated from data given in the *Boletín Económico de América Latina* (November 1961), pp. 17–20.

23. The role of the Chaco War in developing the political consciousness which formed the matrix for the Bolivian Revolution is generally stressed by observers. See, for example, Robert J. Alexander, "Bolivia: The Government and Politics of the National Revolution," in Martin C. Needler (ed.), *Political Systems of Latin America* (Princeton, N.J.: Van Nos-

trand, 1964), p. 323. A similar development began in Paraguay but was frustrated by a combination of circumstances.
Comparable developments, sometimes in weaker form, followed participation in both world wars for the countries of
Europe. Even where violent revolutions did not take place,
the upsurge in popular demands led to the introduction or
vast expansion of social services, with far-reaching significance
for the structure of society.

Chapter Four

1. A series of such pairs of mutually contradictory hypotheses
drawn from the literature is very neatly formulated by Lyle
N. McAlister in his contribution to John J. Johnson (ed.),
Continuity and Change in Latin America (Stanford: Stanford University Press, 1964), pp. 158–159. Some authors
point out the evidence that various mutually opposed tendencies exist without attempting to subsume them in some
general formulation. This is Johnson's own approach, (see
his *The Military and Society in Latin America* [Stanford:
Stanford University Press, 1964], Introduction and Chap. 9)
and also that of Irving Horowitz, in "United States Policy
and the Latin American Military Establishment," *The Cor-
respondent* (Autumn 1964). Lieuwen reconciles opposing
tendencies by means of positing cycles in which a set of
trends in one direction is succeeded by a countervailing set;
see Edwin Lieuwen, *Arms and Politics in Latin America*, rev.
ed. (New York: Praeger, 1961), especially Chap. 5.

2. McAlister argues in favor of this "revisionist" approach, which
regards military intervention as chiefly a response to functional imperatives rather than as an expression of willful
selfishness, in "Changing Concepts of the Role of the Military in Latin America," *The Annals* (July 1965), pp. 90–92.
See also his interesting and helpful survey of the literature,
"Recent Research and Writings on the Role of the Military
in Latin America," *Latin American Research Review* (Fall
1966). But the two views need not be considered mutually
exclusive and representative of antagonistic positions, as Mc-
Alister interprets them; they can, and in this writer's opinion
should, instead be regarded as an expression of the familiar
complementarity of intention and situation, predisposition
and occasion, motive and opportunity. The civilian population, or sectors of it, may demand a military seizure of power

to "save the country from communism," to restore financial stability, to eliminate corruption. A military group may accept the challenge in order to be able to increase the budget for weapons procurement, raise the authorized number of officers in the higher ranks, or crush a political group working for strengthened civilian control.

3. The data on coups d'état used in this chapter were compiled and coded by Walter C. Soderlund. In this chapter no attempt is made to distinguish among different types of extraconstitutional seizures of power, although the author is of course aware that a popular revolt should not properly be referred to as a coup d'état.

4. Edwin Lieuwen discusses the relation between the depression and military intervention in "Militarism and Politics in Latin America," in John J. Johnson (ed.), *The Role of the Military in Underdeveloped Countries* (Princeton, N.J.: Princeton University Press, 1962).

5. It should not be thought that economic conditions worsened as a result of the coup. At least as commonly, in the writer's experience, conditions improve as business confidence shows an upsurge after a coup, which normally occurs without appreciable economic dislocation and typically removes a government regarded as incompetent.

6. Víctor Alba, "The Stages of Militarism in Latin America," in John J. Johnson (ed.), *The Role of the Military in Underdeveloped Countries, op. cit.*, p. 165.

7. Admiral Ramón Castro Jijón, quoted in the *Diario Las Américas* (Miami), May 28, 1964. For a detailed account of the creation of an interventionist frame of mind on the part of the military, see Martin C. Needler, *Anatomy of a Coup d'Etat: Ecuador, 1963* (Washington, D.C.: Institute for the Comparative Study of Political Systems, 1964), Chap. 5. Johnson gives a Brazilian example of civilians publicly inciting the military to revolt on p. 124 of his *The Role of the Military in Underdeveloped Countries*. Juan Bosch, who is in a good position to know about such things, comments: "In the Dominican Republic, the most influential strata of the population joined with political leaders . . . They worked assiduously in the barracks to induce the soldiers to undertake the coup of September 25, 1963." *The Unfinished Experiment: Democracy in the Dominican Republic* (New York: Praeger, 1965), p. xi. S. E. Finer discusses the interventionist mood in *The Man on Horseback* (New York: Praeger, 1963), Chap. 5.

8. For one such case of which the author has personal knowledge, see his *Anatomy of a Coup d'Etat: Ecuador, 1963, op. cit.,* p. 19.

9. This is also Lieuwen's view: "On the balance, the armed forces have been a force for the preservation of the *status quo;* their political intervention has generally signified, as it does today, a conservative action . . ." Edwin Lieuwen, "The Military: A Force for Continuity or Change," in John TePaske and Sydney N. Fisher (eds.), *Explosive Forces in Latin America* (Columbus: Ohio State University Press, 1964), p. 77.

10. It is the conclusion of Lieuwen's insightful *Generals Vs. Presidents* (New York: Praeger, 1964), pp. 101–107, that the last factor mentioned has been the crucial one in the recent coups.

11. The following successful insurrections took place during the period:

    Argentina: June 1943, February 1944, September 1955, March 1962

    Bolivia: May 1936, July 1937, December 1943, July 1946, May 1951, April 1952, November 1964

    Brazil: October 1945, August 1954, November 1955, April 1964

    Colombia: June 1953, May 1957

    Costa Rica: March 1948

    Cuba: March 1952, January 1959

    Dominican Republic: September 1963

    Ecuador: August 1935, October 1937, May 1944, August 1947, November 1961, July 1963

    El Salvador: May 1944, October 1944, December 1948, October 1960, January 1961

    Guatemala: July 1944, October 1944, June 1954, March 1963

    Haiti: January 1946, May 1950, December 1956

    Honduras: October 1956, October 1963

    Nicaragua: June 1936

    Panama: October 1941, November 1949, May 1951

    Paraguay: February 1936, August 1937, June 1948, January 1949, September 1949, May 1954

    Peru: October 1948, July 1962

    Venezuela: October 1945, November 1948, January 1958

12. The question is stated in this form to facilitate coding.

13. Morris Janowitz, *The Professional Soldier* (New York: Free Press, 1964; first printing, 1960).

14. Medina Echevarría states flatly that the officers seizing power today "come, practically without exception, from hard-working middle-class families." José Medina Echevarría and Benjamin Higgins, *Social Aspects of Economic Development in Latin America* (Paris: UNESCO, 1963), II, 88.

15. The evidence for these developments is summarized by Edwin Lieuwen, *Arms and Politics in Latin America*, rev. ed. (New York: Praeger, 1961), pp. 122–153. If one thought solely in terms of these factors, as some authors do, regarding military political activity exclusively as being "pushed" by pressures internal to the military, rather than being also "pulled" by the demands of the total political situation, then it would be logical to expect these changes to result in greater professionalism and technicism, reducing military involvement in politics, and in greater sympathy with the lower classes, rendering such involvement more progressive in orientation. Although several authors have assumed viewpoints of this type, they do not appear substantiated by the evidence cited above.

16. The concept of "weight" is discussed below.

17. This has been found true also in the case of the Turkish coup of 1960. See Ergun Özbudun, *The Role of the Military in Recent Turkish Politics*, Occasional Paper No. 14 (Cambridge, Mass.: Harvard Center for International Affairs, November 1966), p. 35.

18. This set of dynamics is of course not peculiar to Latin America. Classic occupants of the role of "swing man," with local variations, have been Naguib in Egypt, Gürsel in Turkey, Chehab in Lebanon, and Aguiyi-Ironsi in Nigeria—perhaps even de Gaulle in France. Of General Gürsel, Özbudun writes, "Gürsel was not one of the instigators of the conspiracy, and he played almost no role in the planning and execution of the coup. He was chosen to head the NUC because of the fear of the younger revolutionaries that they might not be able to command the loyalty of their superiors unless they worked under the leadership of a popular and highly respected general." *Ibid.*, p. 10.

19. "Man in the News," *The New York Times*, April 6, 1964. Typographic errors in the original have been corrected.

20. See Arthur Whitaker, *Argentine Upheaval* (New York: Praeger, 1956); Lieuwen, *Generals Vs. Presidents, op. cit.*, pp. 10–25; James W. Rowe, *The Argentine Elections of 1963: An Analysis* (Washington: Institute for the Compara-

tive Study of Political Systems, n.d.), pp. 11–18; Peter G. Snow, "Parties and Politics in Argentina: The Elections of 1962 and 1963," *Midwest Journal of Political Science* (February 1965).

21. See Lieuwen, *Generals Vs. Presidents, op. cit.,* pp. 69–85, and Phyllis Peterson, "Brazil: Institutionalized Confusion," in Martin C. Needler (ed.), *Political Systems of Latin America* (Princeton, N.J.: Van Nostrand, 1964), pp. 473–477.

22. See Lieuwen, *General Vs. Presidents, op. cit.,* pp. 26–36, and Martin C. Needler, "Peru Since the *Coup d'Etat,*" *The World Today* (February 1963).

23. In one variant of this situation, the provisional president may save his own personal position by switching sides at the last minute and adopting the program of the "hard liners," if the forces they can marshal seem decisive. This tactic was adopted by Castelo Branco in early 1966.

24. It is of course possible, as Edwin Martin and others have pointed out in communications to the author, that coups are more likely to be directed against constitutional governments because more such governments are in office.

25. The author has discussed it in "United States Recognition Policy and the Peruvian Case," *Inter-American Economic Affairs* (Spring 1963).

Chapter Five

1. This is not to say that the Hispanic tradition has no political significance. Of course it has such significance, and we are badly in need of studies which handle the question with rigor and discrimination, instead of using the cultural tradition as a diffuse, all-purpose, "lazy man's" explanation of everything.

2. Bruce Russett, *et al.,* *World Handbook of Political and Social Indicators* (New Haven, Conn.: Yale University Press, 1964), pp. 295–297.

3. A. F. K. Organski, *The Stages of Political Development* (New York: Knopf, 1965).

4. For those who wish to pursue the ranking game further, the writer would suggest the interesting (although not comparable) rankings given by Edwin Lieuwen in *Arms and Politics in Latin America,* rev. ed. (New York: Praeger, 1961), pp. 158–171; Samuel Shapiro, *Invisible Latin America* (Boston:

Beacon Press, 1963), Chap. 2; Karl Schmitt and David D. Burks, *Evolution or Chaos: The Dynamics of Latin American Politics* (New York: Praeger, 1963), pp. 175–178. See also Peter G. Snow, "A Scalogram Analysis of Political Development," *The American Behavioral Scientist* (March 1966), p. 35.

5. Seymour Martin Lipset, *Political Man: The Social Basis of Politics* (New York: Anchor Books, 1963), pp. 27–63.

6. Gabriel Almond and James S. Coleman, *The Politics of the Developing Areas* (Princeton, N.J.: Princeton University Press, 1960), p. 541.

7. See Russell H. Fitzgibbon and Kenneth F. Johnson, "Measurement of Latin American Political Change," *American Political Science Review* (September 1961), p. 525.

8. As Lipset points out, *op. cit.*, p. 31n.

9. Charles Wolf, Jr., "The Political Effects of Economic Programs: Some Indications from Latin America," *Economic Development and Cultural Change* (October 1965).

10. Phillips Cutright, "National Political Development: Its Measurement and Social Correlates," reprinted in Nelson W. Polsby, Robert A. Dentler, and Paul A. Smith (eds.), *Politics and Social Life: An Introduction to Political Behavior* (Boston: Houghton Mifflin, 1963).

11. Bruce M. Russett, *et al.*, *World Handbook of Political and Social Indicators* (New Haven, Conn.: Yale University Press, 1964), pp. 320–321.

12. Using figures from P. N. Rosenstein-Rodan, "International Aid for Underdeveloped Countries," *The Review of Economics and Statistics* (May 1961). Figures are estimates for 1961 in real terms. Slight changes in rank orderings, but not differing consistently in any one direction, are obtained by using other sets of gross national product figures or other economic development indices.

13. See Karl W. Deutsch, "Social Mobilization and Political Development," *American Political Science Review* (September 1961).

14. Published sets of figures on electoral participation have a marked tendency to unreliability. Thus the table given in the *Statistical Abstract of Latin America* for 1964 (Los Angeles and Berkeley: University of California Press, 1965) on electoral participation is incomplete; the author has not checked all of the figures that it gives, and many agree with those given by Labelle and Estrada and used here, but two

of them are patently false: the Nicaraguan figure of an electoral participation of 80 percent of the population is surely
extraordinary since only some 50 percent of the population
are of voting age; and, apparently due to an error in computation, the Chilean turnout was reported as 55 percent,
when the correct figure should have been about one-third
of that. Russett's electoral participation table gives turnout
as a percentage of voting age population, rather than the
whole population; the raw figures are not given, so the com-
putations cannot be checked, but at least one figure, that
given for Paraguay, is patently false, and other computation
errors may have crept in. Russett, *et al., op. cit.*, pp. 84–85.

15. It is worthy of note that of the seven cases in which the
economic development index—that is, the rank ordering on
life expectancy—falls outside the range between the constitutionality and the participation rank orderings in Table 7, only
one of these cases, that of Bolivia, seems to the author to
constitute a genuine exception to the hypothesis posited.
The seven cases will be examined in turn.

One of them is, of course, Cuba, where the rank orderings
on constitutionality, economic development, and participation respectively are 12–3–10. Here the participation ranking
is much lower than the hypothesis would predict; however,
this is only to be expected, since the ranking given, in the
absence of a free election, is that of the most recent election, that of 1954, which was notoriously rigged and the
outcome (that of the "election" of the incumbent Batista)
was known beforehand. If Fidel Castro were overthrown
tomorrow and free elections held, the author would antici-
pate a high turnout figure comparable to those shown in
Venezuela or the Dominican Republic.

In the case of Paraguay, where the rank orderings run
18–8–10, it is clearly the middle figure, that for life expectancy, which must be suspect. Paraguayan statistics may
be the worst in Latin America, but in any case if Paraguay
is indeed eighth in life expectancy among the Latin American countries, that is the only social or economic indicator
on which it reaches eighth place; on other economic indicators, Paraguay ranges between twelfth and eighteenth
place.

In four of the remaining five cases the economic development indicator falls only slightly outside of the predicted
range: on Panama the rank orderings are 5–5–11; on Hon-

duras 13–15–13; on El Salvador 16–14–16; and on Uruguay 2–1–3.

Only the case of Bolivia, with rank orderings of 9–20–8, constitutes an unequivocal exception to the hypothesis postulated. This remains true even if it is acknowledged that constitutional stability in Bolivia during this period has probably been overrated, due to especially acute coding problems. The problem can be stated clearly: the participation and constitutionality indices indicate that Bolivia is politically a relatively developed country, yet at the same time it remains economically extremely backward. Clearly Bolivia has been mobilized politically by some means other than economic change. The explanation for this has, however, already been advanced in Chapter Three: in Bolivia the Indians were mobilized and were given a sense of personal efficacy usually found among occupants of higher-status positions in more developed societies, by having been enlisted into combat during the Chaco War. In other words, political development is correlated with economic development because the latter produces effects (presumably higher levels of organization and communications, greater "sense of efficacy," and so forth) that support the former. But these effects can also be produced, without economic development, by other causes, such as recruitment into combat. It is thus likely that thirty years ago, before the Mexican economy had developed to its present point, the rank orderings for Mexico would have shown a similar inconsistency, since the processes of change at work in Mexico resemble those operating more recently in Bolivia.

16. This may also be formulated as the principle that political development and economic development are aspects of a single process, the position taken by Hélio Jaguaribe in his *Desenvolvimento econômico e desenvolvimento político* (Rio de Janeiro: Editôra Fundo de Cultura, 1962).

17. This conclusion appears to be confirmed by attitude survey data from Chile and Argentina turned up by the project headed by Alex Inkeles and still in progress at the time of writing: that as the propensity to participate in politics increases, support for the existing political order tends to decrease. It is also foreshadowed in a remarkable passage by Karl Deutsch: "Such mobilization, however, is usually accompanied by rising needs and expectations, which must not be frustrated if stability is to be preserved . . . In principle,

the background conditions for stability—though not stability itself—could be predicted from a ratio of two numbers: one indicating the rising burdens upon a government and upon popular habits of compliance or loyalty toward it; the other indicating the resources available to the government for coping with these burdens." Deutsch goes on to develop a rather complex formula to express these relations, with political participation a component of the indicator of "rising burdens." Deutsch, op. cit., p. 39.

18. The formulation of Claude Ake appears to be comparable. See A Theory of Political Integration (Homewood, Ill.: Dorsey, 1967), p. 15.

19. It should be clearly understood that explaining relationships at this aggregative level does not preclude their simultaneous explanation at other levels, such as that of individual psychology. Individuals vote, or refrain from voting, for all kinds of reasons, for example; but the aggregate level of availability of motives to vote or abstain is a resultant of forces operating at the level of the whole society.

20. These figures are given in The Chilean Presidential Election of September 4, 1964, Part II (Washington, D.C.: Institute for the Comparative Study of Political Systems, 1965), p. 2.

21. This point is spelled out in detail by Willard F. Barber and C. Neale Ronning in their Internal Security and Military Power: Counterinsurgency and Civic Action in Latin America (Columbus: Ohio State University Press, 1966), pp. 40–41.

22. This point is discussed in Martin C. Needler, Latin American Politics in Perspective (Princeton, N.J.: Van Nostrand, 1963), p. 18.

23. Fred W. Riggs has pointed out to the writer the parallelism with the growth of economic welfare, which is likewise subject to tension—between the requirements of economic growth, on the one hand, and demands for more equitable distribution of the product, on the other.

Chapter Six

1. Charles Wagley, "On the Concept of Social Race in the Americas," in Dwight B. Heath and Richard N. Adams (eds.), Contemporary Cultures and Societies of Latin America (New York: Random House, 1965), pp. 531–544.

2. The anthropological literature is rich in evidence on this point. See, for example, Richard N. Adams, *A Community in the Andes: Problems and Progress in Muquiyauyo* (Seattle: University of Washington Press, 1959), pp. 84 ff. Adams writes that in Muquiyauyo social distinctions between "Indian" and "mestizo" are maintained even though, strictly speaking, the population is "racially" all mestizo. For an interesting discussion of the identification of socioracial groups and "status" groups, see Norman E. Whitten, Jr., *Class, Kinship, and Power in an Ecuadorian Town: The Negroes of San Lorenzo* (Stanford: Stanford University Press, 1965), *passim*, especially Chap. 5. Richard W. Patch has written of the "fiction of ethnic difference of the 'Indian' or *serrano*." "La Parada, Lima's Market. Part II: *Serrano* and *Criollo*, the Confusion of Race with Class," American Universities Field Service Reports, West Coast South America Series, Vol. XIV, No. 2 (February 1967).

3. Countries are considered "European" if their population is over 85 percent of European ancestry; "Indian" if, after 1900, more than 30 percent of the population still spoke an Indian language; otherwise, either "mestizo" or "mulatto," depending on whether the mixed European-Indian or the European-African element is more important in determining social structure. Haiti, the only Latin American country almost exclusively of unmixed African ancestry, might have constituted a category by itself, but has been included in the mulatto category. Chile might be regarded as belonging to the European rather than the mestizo category, but the mestizo designation is probably more accurate. The opposite decision has been made in the case of Costa Rica, which is also somewhat ambiguous. Mexico is generally considered today a mestizo country, but the homogeneous national culture to which this designation generally refers is relatively recent and still only partial. In any case, if Chile is a mestizo society, it comes closest of all those in that category to the economic standards of the European group; while Mexico, similarly, is the closest of the Indian group to the mestizo levels. Thus the socioracial ambiguity is still accurately reflected in the economic figures. Panama is both mestizo and mulatto; but the mulatto element is more dominant in the key cities and seems more critical in determining national social structure. A similar comment can be made of Venezuela; the reverse holds true of Colombia.

4. It is interesting to note that in a situation where virtually all of the broad socioracial groups present in Latin America are represented, the prestige ranking appears to follow this ranking of the different types of society by social and economic level. In San Lorenzo, "whites" and lighter mestizos and mulattoes had more social prestige, while among construction workers, "In general, the mestizos and the Negroes regarded each other more or less as equals, and both looked upon the Indian, set apart by his non-Western dress, as inferior." Whitten, op. cit., p. 31.

5. Russett has data on only four of the Latin American countries; Bruce Russett, et al., World Handbook of Political and Social Indicators (New Haven, Conn.: Yale University Press, 1964), p. 245.

6. The inequality of social conditions in Chile has most recently been discussed, with supporting statistics, in Federico G. Gil and Charles J. Parrish, The Chilean Presidential Election of September 4, 1964, Part I (Washington, D.C.: Institute for the Comparative Study of Political Systems, 1965), pp. 10–11. Data on inequality in Colombia have most recently been provided by Milton C. Taylor and Raymond L. Richman, "Public Finance and Development in Colombia," Journal of Inter-American Studies (January 1966), pp. 11–12.

7. William T. Mangin, "Mental Health and Migration in Cities: A Peruvian Case," in Heath and Adams (eds.), op. cit., p. 551.

8. Everett Hagen, On the Theory of Social Change (Homewood, Ill.: Dorsey, 1962), pp. 204–205.

9. This is pointed out by William P. Glade, "Revolution and Economic Development," in W. P. Glade and C. W. Anderson, The Political Economy of Mexico (Madison: University of Wisconsin Press, 1963), p. 38.

10. See Hagen, op. cit., p. 213.

11. George I. Blanksten, Ecuador: Constitutions and Caudillos (Berkeley and Los Angeles: University of California Press, 1948).

12. See the discussion of this point in Martin C. Needler, Latin American Politics in Perspective (Princeton, N.J.: Van Nostrand, 1963), p. 85.

13. Andrew Whiteford, Two Cities of Latin America (New York: Anchor Books, 1964).

14. Daniel Goldrich, "Toward the Comparative Study of Poli-

ticization in Latin America," in Heath and Adams (eds.), *op. cit.*, pp. 361–378.

15. *Mensaje a la nación del General René Barrientos Ortuño, Presidente Constitucional de la República, 6 de agosto de 1966* (La Paz: Dirección de Prensa e Informaciones, Presidencia de la República, 1966), p. 79.

16. *The Chilean Presidential Election of September 4, 1964,* Part II (Washington, D.C.: Institute for the Comparative Study of Political Systems, 1965), p. 2.

17. Moreover, Aldo E. Solari has shown that in Uruguay party loyalty is strongest in the economically less developed areas. "Impacto político de las diferencias internas de los países en los grados e índices de modernización y desarrollo económico en América Latina," *América Latina* (January–March 1965), p. 12.

18. Charles W. Anderson, "Nicaragua: The Somoza Dynasty," in Martin C. Needler (ed.), *Political Systems of Latin America* (Princeton, N.J.: Van Nostrand, 1964), p. 98.

19. Richard S. Weinert, "Violence in Pre-Modern Societies: Rural Colombia," *American Political Science Review* (June 1966). See also Malcolm Deas, "Politics and Violence: Aspects of 'La Violencia' in Colombia," *Encounter* (September 1965).

20. See Mario C. Vázquez, "Changes in the Social Stratification of an Andean Hacienda," in Heath and Adams (eds.), *op. cit.*, pp. 405–423.

Chapter Seven

1. Each of these statements is of course least true about Haiti, which consistently shows the greatest variations from Latin American patterns from the colonial period on.

2. For a strong statement of this position, see Orlando Albornoz, *Libertad académica y educación superior en América Latina* (Caracas: Dipuven, 1966), p. 13.

3. Adam Ulam, *The Unfinished Revolution* (New York: Random House, 1964).

4. See Theodore Draper's *Castroism: Theory and Practice* (New York: Praeger, 1965).

5. "The Latin American army officer, particularly one of high rank, has since Independence always been in the upper social stratum, however plebeian his origin." Robert J. Alexander, "The Army in Politics," in Harold E. Davis (ed.),

Government and Politics in Latin America (New York: Ronald Press, 1958), p. 154.

6. This is not to say that military officers invariably play a conservative role; they do not. They are more likely than not to play such a role during a period of evolutionary innovation, however.

7. The attitude of the Venezuelan military to the Betancourt government is discussed in Robert J. Alexander, *The Venezuelan Democratic Revolution* (New Brunswick: Rutgers University Press, 1964), pp. 116–117.

8. This is a probability but not an unfailing truth. Occasionally a country may have prestige not because of its advanced level of social, economic, or political development but because of cultural or religious characteristics which lend it special moral authority.

9. This has been demonstrated empirically by Thomas Schelling, as described in his *Strategy of Conflict* (New York: Oxford University Press, 1963).

10. This has been very nicely put by Anthony Wedgwood Benn: "The history of the British ruling class is the history of judicious retreats in the face of the inevitable. A mixture of realism, humanity, and laziness has saved them from the gallows and us from the barricades." "Reform in the Air," *Manchester Guardian Weekly*, April 16, 1964.

11. To use Samuel Beer's terms.

12. The process of constitution making itself implies prior agreement, explicit or implicit, voluntary or coerced, establishing procedures and committing the participants to abide by the result. This fundamental agreement may be brought about by the presence of an occupying power which has stipulated certain ground rules under which the bargaining shall take place, as in post-World War II Germany; or it may derive from acute awareness of the dangers that failure to reach a viable decision would entail: renewal of civil war, inability to defend the state against foreign enemies, or economic collapse. The elements representing different interests or points of view can be weighted differently in the discussions: each equally, each according to the numbers of people it represents, or each according to the military capabilities of which it would dispose if fighting were renewed.

13. Compare Samuel P. Huntington, "Political Development and Political Decay," *World Politics* (April 1965), pp. 400–401.

Chapter Eight

1. C. W. Cassinelli, *The Politics of Freedom: An Analysis of the Modern Democratic State* (Seattle: University of Washington Press, 1961), especially Chap. 4.
2. *Ibid.*, Chap. 3.
3. *Ibid.*, p. 67.
4. "Indeed, the only agreement which is essential is the agreement on the elements of constitutionalism." Carl J. Friedrich, *The New Belief in the Common Man* (Boston: Little, Brown, 1942), p. 165.
5. A. D. Lindsay, *The Modern Democratic State* (London: Oxford University Press, 1959); Henry B. Mayo, *An Introduction to Democratic Theory* (New York: Oxford University Press, 1960); Robert A. Dahl and Charles E. Lindblom, *Politics, Economics and Welfare* (New York: Harper & Row, 1953); Cassinelli, *op. cit.*; Thomas L. Thorsen, *The Logic of Democracy* (New York: Holt, Rinehart and Winston, 1962).
6. Friedrich's point is thus well taken that the stress on the desirability of a high order of substantive consensus is outside the mainstream of democratic thought.
7. The problem has not yet reached an acute stage on the Continent, although a chauvinistic organization in Geneva has reportedly sought to find evidence of popular support for its exclusionist position by polling the public and asking such questions as "Would you want your daughter to marry a Sicilian?"
8. On the "asynchrony" of development, see the interesting remarks of J. Roland Pennock, "Political Development, Political Systems, and Political Goods," *World Politics* (April 1966), pp. 416–418. The point is also dealt with by Gino Germani in *Política y sociedad en una epoca de transición* (Buenos Aires: Editorial Paidos, 1962), pp. 98–101.
9. Samuel P. Huntington, "Political Development and Political Decay," *World Politics* (April 1965). However, in a later article Huntington adds the expansion of participation as a third dimension of "political modernization" to two formal dimensions: rationalization of authority and differentiation of function and structure. "Political Development: America Vs. Europe," *World Politics* (April 1966).
10. Different types of short-run relationships between economic

and political development are explored in Charles Wolf, Jr., "The Political Effects of Economic Programs: Some Indications from Latin America," *Economic Development and Cultural Change* (October 1965), pp. 1–8.

11. An ideology of economic nationalism may serve as a functional equivalent for coercion in maintaining stability while sacrifices are being exacted from the lower classes; Harry G. Johnson has suggested that policies of economic nationalism are accompanied by the redistribution of income from the lower to the middle classes. "A Theoretical Model of Economic Nationalism in New and Developing States," *Political Science Quarterly* (June 1965).

12. For a citation of some relevant studies on this point, see H. M. Phillips, "Conclusion," in José Medina Echeverría and Benjamin Higgins, *Social Aspects of Economic Development in Latin America* (Paris: UNESCO, 1963), II, 264.

13. It can be noted parenthetically that the same linguistic confusion vitiates much commentary on the political significance of social class in other countries. In Great Britain, for example, the classes in the middle of the socioeconomic structure are skilled workers, technicians, foremen, and the poorer self-employed, rather than the so-called middle class. Failure to appreciate this makes nonsense, for example, of John Bonham's *The Middle Class Vote* (London: Faber and Faber, 1954). Bonham tries to show that the balance of power between the two major parties in Britain does not lie with middle groups in the socioeconomic structure by demonstrating that it does not lie with the "middle class." A reanalysis of the figures Bonham uses, without falling into the semantic trap, suggests conclusions diametrically opposed to those Bonham draws, however.

14. A "revolution" with conservative intent, to complete the symmetry, can also draw its strength from people who are political participants but whose status is threatened as a result of general economic deterioration or structural change. This type of person formed the core of Hitler's support, of course, and was deliberately sought out by him. See Martin C. Needler, "Hitler's Anti-Semitism: a Political Appraisal," *Public Opinion Quarterly* (Winter 1960).

15. Everett E. Hagen, *On the Theory of Social Change* (Homewood, Ill.: Dorsey, 1962), p. 86.

16. On this point, the work of M. Brewster Smith and his associates is particularly instructive. See M. B. Smith, Jerome

S. Bruner, and Robert W. White, *Opinions and Personality* (New York: Wiley, 1956). See also Herbert C. Kelman, "Compliance, Identification, and Internalization: Three Processes of Attitude Change," reprinted from the *Journal of Conflict Resolution* in J. David Singer (ed.), *Human Behavior and International Relations* (Chicago: Rand McNally, 1965), pp. 232–234.

17. The problem of the relation between explanations of the same phenomenon at different levels of analysis is interestingly discussed by Silvia Sigal and Eliseo Verón, "Notas sobre las relaciones entre psicología y sociología," *Revista Latinoamericana de Sociología*, Vol. 65, No. 2 (July 1965).

18. Gabriel A. Almond and Sidney Verba, *The Civic Culture*, abr. ed. (Boston: Little, Brown, 1965), especially p. 173.

Conclusion

1. The ideological, as well as the economic, factors involved in the abolition of slavery should be mentioned here.

2. See Leonard Kasden, "Family Structure, Migration, and the Entrepreneur" (following Gerald Brennan), *Comparative Studies in Society and History* (July 1965), p. 349.

Selected Bibliography on Political Development, with Special Reference to Latin America

Books

Ake, Claude. A *Theory of Political Integration*. Homewood, Ill.: Dorsey, 1967.

Almond, Gabriel, and James S. Coleman (eds.). *The Politics of the Developing Areas*. Princeton, N.J.: Princeton University Press, 1960.

————, and G. Bingham Powell. *Comparative Politics: A Developmental Approach*. Boston: Little, Brown, 1966.

————, and Sidney Verba. *The Civic Culture: Political Attitudes and Democracy in Five Nations*. Princeton, N.J.: Princeton University Press, 1963.

Anderson, Charles W. *Politics and Economic Change in Latin America*. Princeton, N.J.: Van Nostrand, 1967.

Baklanoff, Eric (ed.). *New Perspectives of Brazil*. Nashville, Tenn.: Vanderbilt University Press, 1966.

Barber, Willard F., and C. Neale Ronning. *Internal Security and Military Power: Counterinsurgency and Civic Action in Latin America*. Columbus: Ohio State University Press, 1966.

Finer, Samuel E. *The Man on Horseback*. New York: Praeger, 1963.

Finkle, Jason, and Richard Gable (eds.). *Political Development and Social Change*. New York: Wiley, 1967.

Fuentes, Carlos, *et al.* *Whither Latin America?* New York: Monthly Review Press, 1963.

Germani, Gino. *Política y sociedad en una epoca de transición*. Buenos Aires: Editorial Paidos, 1964.

Goldrich, Daniel. *Sons of the Establishment*. Chicago: Rand McNally, 1966.

Hagen, Everett. *On the Theory of Social Change*. Homewood, Ill.: Dorsey, 1962.

Heath, Dwight B., and Richard N. Adams (eds.). *Contemporary Cultures and Societies of Latin America*. New York: Random House, 1965.

Imaz, José Luis de. *La clase alta de Buenos Aires*. Buenos Aires: Instituto de Sociología de la Universidad de Buenos Aires, 1962.

————. *Los que mandan*. Buenos Aires: Eudeba, 1964.

Jaguaribe, Hélio. *Desenvolvimento econômico e desenvolvimento político*. Rio de Janiero: Editôra Fundo de Cultura, 1962.

Jane, Cecil. *Liberty and Despotism in Spanish America*. London: Clarendon, 1929.

Janowitz, Morris. *The Military in the Political Development of New Nations*. Chicago: University of Chicago Press, 1964.

Johnson, Chalmers. *Revolutionary Change*. Boston: Little, Brown, 1967.

Johnson, John J. (ed.). *Continuity and Change in Latin America*. Stanford, Calif.: Stanford University Press, 1964.

———— (ed.). *The Role of the Military in Underdeveloped Countries*. Princeton, N.J.: Princeton University Press, 1962.

————. *The Military and Society in Latin America*. Stanford, Calif.: Stanford University Press, 1964.

LaPalombara, Joseph (ed.). *Bureaucracy and Political Development*. Princeton, N.J.: Princeton University Press, 1963.

————, and Myron Weiner (eds.). *Political Parties and Political Development*. Princeton, N.J.: Princeton University Press, 1966.

Levy, Marion J., Jr. *Modernization and the Structure of Societies*. 2 vols. Princeton, N.J.: Princeton University Press, 1966.

Lieuwen, Edwin. *Arms and Politics in Latin America*. Rev. ed. New York: Praeger, 1961.

Lipset, Seymour Martin. *Political Man: The Social Basis of Politics*. New York: Anchor Books, 1963.

————, and Aldo E. Solari (eds.). *Elites in Latin America*. New York: Oxford University Press, 1967.

Marshall, T. H. *Class, Citizenship and Social Development*. New York: Anchor Books, 1965.

Medina Echevarría, José, and Benjamin Higgins. *Social Aspects of Economic Development in Latin America*. Paris: UNESCO, 1963.

Organski, A. F. K. *The Stages of Political Development*. New York: Knopf, 1965.

Pye, Lucian. *Aspects of Political Development*. Boston: Little, Brown, 1966.

———— (ed.). *Communications and Political Development*. Princeton, N.J.: Princeton University Press, 1961.

Russett, Bruce, *et al. World Handbook of Political and Social Indicators*. New Haven, Conn.: Yale University Press, 1964.

Santa, Eduardo. *Sociología politica de Colombia*. Bogota: Ediciones Tercer Mundo, 1964.

Schmitt, Karl, and David D. Burks. *Evolution or Chaos: The Dynamics of Latin American Politics*. New York: Praeger, 1963.

Shapiro, Samuel. *Invisible Latin America*. Boston: Beacon Press, 1963.

Silvert, Kalman H. *The Conflict Society*. New Orleans: Hauser Press, 1961.

Tannenbaum, Frank. *Ten Keys to Latin America*. New York: Knopf, 1963.

TePaske, John, and Sydney N. Fisher (eds.). *Explosive Forces in Latin America*. Columbus: Ohio State University Press, 1964.

Veliz, Claudio (ed.). *Obstacles to Change in Latin America*. New York: Oxford University Press, 1965.

Williams, Edward J. *Latin American Christian Democratic Parties*. Nashville: University of Tennessee Press, 1967.

Wolf, Charles, Jr. *United States Policy and the Third World*. Boston: Little, Brown, 1967.

Articles and Individual Chapters

Anderson, Charles W. "Toward a Theory of Latin American Politics," Occasional Paper No. 2. Nashville, Tenn.: Graduate Center for Latin American Politics, Vanderbilt University, February 1964.

Angell, Alan. "Party Systems in Latin America," *The Political Quarterly* (July–September 1966).

Cutright, Phillips. "The Measurement of Social Development," reprinted in Nelson W. Polsby, Robert A. Dentler, and Paul A. Smith (eds.), *Politics and Social Life: An Introduction to Political Behavior*. Boston: Houghton Mifflin, 1963.

Fitzgibbon, Russell H., and Kenneth F. Johnson. "Measurement of Latin American Political Change," *American Political Science Review* (September 1961).

Germani, Gino, and Kalman H. Silvert. "Politics, Social Structure, and Military Intervention in Latin America," *European Journal of Sociology*, Vol. 2 (1961).

Huntington, Samuel P. "Political Development and Political Decay," *World Politics* (April 1965).

Inkeles, Alex. "The Modernization of Man," in Myron Weiner (ed.), *Modernization: The Dynamics of Growth*. New York: Basic Books, 1966.

Iutaka, Sugiyama. "Social Stratification Research in Latin America," *Latin American Research Review* (Fall 1965).

Johnson, Harry G. "A Theoretical Model of Economic Nationalism in New and Developing States," *Political Science Quarterly* (June 1965).

Journal of International Affairs, "Political Development in Latin America," special issue of Vol. 20, No. 2, 1966; see especially Alfred Stepan, "Political Development and Theory: the Latin American Experience."

Kling, Merle. "Toward a Theory of Power and Political Instability in Latin America," *Western Political Quarterly* (March 1956).

Mangin, William. "Latin American Squatter Settlements: A Problem and a Solution," *Latin American Research Review* (Summer 1967).

McAlister, Lyle. "Changing Concepts of the Role of the Military in Latin America," *The Annals* (July 1965).

———. "The Military," in John J. Johnson (ed.), *Continuity and Change in Latin America*. Stanford, Calif.: Stanford University Press (1964).

———. "Recent Research and Writings on the Role of the Military in Latin America," *Latin American Research Review* (Fall 1966).

McCamant, John F. "El estudio del desarrollo político: una revisión bibliográfica," *Revista de la Sociedad Interamericana de Planificación* (December 1967).

Morse, Richard. "Urbanization in Latin America," *Latin American Research Review* (Fall 1965).

Needler, Martin C. "Political Development and Military Intervention in Latin America," *American Political Science Review* (September 1966).

———. "The Political Development of Mexico," *American Political Science Review* (June 1961).

Packenham, Robert A. "Approaches to the Study of Political Development," *World Politics* (October 1964).

———. "Political Development Doctrines in the American Foreign Aid Program," *World Politics* (January 1966).

Payne, James. "Peru: The Politics of Structured Violence," *Journal of Politics* (August 1965).

Pearse, Andrew. "Agrarian Change Trends in Latin America," *Latin American Research Review* (Summer 1966).

Pierson, W. W. (ed.). "Pathology of Democracy in Latin America: A Symposium," *American Political Science Review* (March 1950).

Pike, Fredrick B. "Aspects of Class Relations in Chile 1850–1960," *Hispanic American Historical Review* (February 1963).

Powell, John Duncan. "Military Assistance and Militarism in Latin America," *Western Political Quarterly* (June 1965).

Pye, Lucian. "The Concept of Political Development," *The Annals* (March 1965).

———. "The Non-Western Political Process," *Journal of Politics* (August 1958).

Rosenstein-Rodan, Paul N. "International Aid for Underdeveloped Countries," *The Review of Economics and Statistics* (May 1961).

Schaedel, Richard P. "Land Reform Studies," *Latin American Research Review* (Summer 1966).

Snow, Peter G. "A Scalogram Analysis of Political Development," *The American Behavioral Scientist* (March 1966).

Solari, Aldo E. "Impacto político de las diferencias internas de los países en los grados e índices de modernización y desarrollo económico en América Latina," *América Latina* (January–March 1965).

Stokes, William S. "Violence as a Power Factor in Latin American Politics," *Western Political Quarterly* (September 1952).

Vekemans, Roger, and J. L. Segundo. "Essay of a Socio-Economic Typology of the Latin American Countries," reprinted in Peter G. Snow (ed.), *Government and Politics in Latin America*. New York: Holt, Rinehart and Winston, 1967.

Wagley, Charles W. "On the Concept of Social Race in the Americas," reprinted in Dwight B. Heath and Richard N. Adams (eds.), *Contemporary Cultures and Societies in Latin America*. New York: Random House, 1965.

———, and Marvin Harris. "A Typology of Latin American Subcultures," reprinted in Dwight B. Heath and Richard N. Adams (eds.), *Contemporary Cultures and Societies of Latin America*. New York: Random House, 1965.

Weinert, Richard S. "Violence in Pre-Modern Societies: Rural Colombia," *American Political Science Review* (September 1961).

Wolf, Charles, Jr. "The Political Effects of Economic Programs: Some Indicators from Latin America," *Economic Development and Cultural Change* (October 1965).

Wolfe, Marshall. "Rural Settlement Patterns and Social Change in Latin America: Notes for a Strategy of Rural Development," *Latin American Research Review* (Spring 1966).

Index

Publications Written Under the Auspices of the Center for International Affairs, Harvard University

Books

The Soviet Bloc, by Zbigniew K. Brzezinski (jointly with the Russian Research Center), 1960. Harvard University Press. Revised edition, 1967.

The Necessity for Choice, by Henry A. Kissinger, 1961. Harper & Bros.

Strategy and Arms Control, by Thomas C. Schelling and Morton H. Halperin, 1961. Twentieth Century Fund.

Rift and Revolt in Hungary, by Ferenc A. Váli, 1961. Harvard University Press.

United States Manufacturing Investment in Brazil, by Lincoln Gordon and Engelbert L. Grommers, 1962. Harvard Business School.

The Economy of Cyprus, by A. J. Meyer, with Simos Vassiliou (jointly with the Center for Middle Eastern Studies), 1962. Harvard University Press.

Entrepreneurs of Lebanon, by Yusif A. Sayigh (jointly with the Center for Middle Eastern Studies), 1962. Harvard University Press.

Communist China 1955–1959: Policy Documents with Analysis, with a Foreword by Robert R. Bowie and John K. Fairbank (jointly with the East Asian Research Center), 1962. Harvard University Press.

In Search of France, by Stanley Hoffmann, Charles P. Kindleberger, Laurence Wylie, Jesse R. Pitts, Jean-Baptiste Duroselle, and François Goguel, 1963. Harvard University Press.

Somali Nationalism, by Saadia Touval, 1963. Harvard University Press.

The Dilemma of Mexico's Development, by Raymond Vernon, 1963. Harvard University Press.

Limited War in the Nuclear Age, by Morton H. Halperin, 1963. John Wiley & Sons.

The Arms Debate, by Robert A. Levine, 1963. Harvard University Press.

Africans on the Land, by Montague Yudelman, 1964. Harvard University Press.

Counterinsurgency Warfare, by David Galula, 1964. Frederick A. Praeger.

People and Policy in the Middle East, by Max Weston Thornburg, 1964. W. W. Norton.

Shaping the Future, by Robert R. Bowie, 1964. Columbia University Press.

Foreign Aid and Foreign Policy, by Edward S. Mason (jointly with the Council on Foreign Relations), 1964. Harper & Row.

Public Policy and Private Enterprise in Mexico, by Miguel S. Wionczek, David H. Shelton, Calvin P. Blair, and Rafael Izquierdo, ed. Raymond Vernon, 1964. Harvard University Press.

How Nations Negotiate, by Fred C. Iklé, 1964. Harper & Row.

China and the Bomb, by Morton H. Halperin (jointly with the East Asian Research Center), 1965. Frederick A. Praeger.

Democracy in Germany, by Fritz Erler (Jodidi Lectures), 1965. Harvard University Press.

The Troubled Partnership, by Henry A. Kissinger (jointly with the Council on Foreign Relations), 1965. McGraw-Hill Book Company.

The Rise of Nationalism in Central Africa, by Robert I. Rotberg, 1965. Harvard University Press.

Pan-Africanism and East African Integration, by Joseph S. Nye, Jr., 1965. Harvard University Press.

Communist China and Arms Control, by Morton H. Halperin and Dwight H. Perkins (jointly with the East Asian Research Center), 1965. Frederick A. Praeger.

Problems of National Strategy, ed. Henry Kissinger, 1965. Frederick A. Praeger.

Deterrence before Hiroshima: The Airpower Background of Modern Strategy, by George H. Quester, 1966. John Wiley & Sons.

Containing the Arms Race, by Jeremy J. Stone, 1966. M.I.T. Press.

Germany and the Atlantic Alliance: The Interaction of Strategy and Politics, by James L. Richardson, 1966. Harvard University Press.

Arms and Influence, by Thomas C. Schelling, 1966. Yale University Press.

Political Change in a West African State, by Martin L. Kilson, 1966. Harvard University Press.

Planning Without Facts: Lessons in Resource Allocation from Nigeria's Development, by Wolfgang F. Stolper, 1966. Harvard University Press.

Export Instability and Economic Development, by Alasdair I. MacBean, 1966. Harvard University Press.

Foreign Policy and Democratic Politics, by Kenneth N. Waltz (jointly with the Institute of War and Peace Studies, Columbia University), 1967. Little, Brown.

Contemporary Military Strategy, by Morton ,H. Halperin, 1967. Little, Brown.

Sino-Soviet Relations and Arms Control, ed. Morton H. Halperin (jointly with the East Asian Research Center), 1967. M.I.T. Press.

Africa and United States Policy, by Rupert Emerson, 1967. Prentice-Hall.

Europe's Postwar Growth, by Charles P. Kindleberger, 1967. Harvard University Press.

The Rise and Decline of the Cold War, by Paul Seabury, 1967. Basic Books.

Student Politics, ed. Seymour Martin Lipset, 1967. Basic Books.

Pakistan's Development: Social Goals and Private Incentives, by Gustav F. Papanek, 1967. Harvard University Press.

Strike a Blow and Die: A Narrative of Race Relations in Colonial Africa, by George Simeon Mwase. Edited and introduced by Robert I. Rotberg, 1967. Harvard University Press.

Aid, Influence, and Foreign Policy, by Joan M. Nelson, 1968. Macmillan.

International Regionalism, by Joseph S. Nye, 1968. Little, Brown.

The TFX Decision: McNamara and the Military, by Robert J. Art, 1968. Little, Brown.

Korea: The Politics of the Vortex, by Gregory Henderson, 1968. Harvard University Press.

Political Development in Latin America: Instability, Violence, and Evolutionary Change, by Martin C. Needler, 1968. Random House.

Occasional Papers Published by the Center for International Affairs

1. *A Plan for Planning: The Need for a Better Method of Assisting Underdeveloped Countries on Their Economic Policies,* by Gustav F. Papanek, 1961. Out of print.
2. *The Flow of Resources from Rich to Poor,* by Alan D. Neale, 1961.
3. *Limited War: An Essay on the Development of the Theory and an Annotated Bibliography,* by Morton H. Halperin, 1962. Out of print.
4. *Reflections on the Failure of the First West Indian Federation,* by Hugh W. Springer, 1962. Out of print.
5. *On the Interaction of Opposing Forces Under Possible Arms Agreements,* by Glenn A. Kent. 1963.